The Ownership Spirit Handbook

Table of Contents

3   The Othello Principle
51   The Owner/Victim Choice
113   Tough-Minded Ownership

Copyright 2003 Quma Learning Systems

This handbook is copyrighted material. All rights reserved. It is against the law to make copies of this material without getting specific written permission in advance from Quma Learning Systems, Inc. No part of this publication may be reproduced, stored in a retrieval system, or transmitted in any form or by any means, electronic, mechanical photocopying, recording or otherwise, without prior written permission from the publisher.

International rights and foreign translations available only through negotiation with Quma Learning Systems, Inc.

Printed in the United States of America

ISBN 1-881840-10-7

Quma Learning Systems, Inc.

800.622.6463 or 480.545.8311

www.quma.net

The Othello Principle

The Eye Sees What the Mind Looks For

The Othello Principle Objectives

Deepen understanding of the value of cultivating an Ownership Spirit

Acquire the benefits and advantages that stem from up-grading mental discipline

Expand understanding and application of The Othello Principle—the impact of consciously-designed perception on performance

Examine case studies of the Othello Principle in action
(Individual and Organizational examples)

Employ the Othello Principle as a tool for
Continuous Self-Diagnosis and Self-Improvement

The Othello Principle
The Eye Sees What the Mind Looks For

Table of Contents

4	The Othello Principle Objectives
7	Degrees of Ownership
10	The Genesis of Ownership
14	Minding the Gap
19	The Othello Principle
29	Real World Examples
35	Self-Diagnosis and Self-Improvement
43	The Assessor

Degrees of Ownership

"The price of greatness is responsibility."
Winston Churchill

*Two brothers, Rick and Charles,
sons of alcoholic parents, were both raised in
the same severely dysfunctional home.*

Charles, the younger brother, is also an alcoholic

"How could I not be?" he asks, using his question as more of a defense than an explanation of his destructive behavior. "Alcoholism is in my genes. Whatever part of my life that's not rolled up in that package is taken care of by the environment I was raised in. It's hard not to learn to be an alcoholic when you're immersed in that lifestyle from the time you're born." Hard? Granted. But Charles has confused "hard not to" with "inevitable" or "impossible not to."

The answer to Charles' question, "How could I not be?" stands next to him in the family portrait. Rick, the older brother, is *not* an alcoholic. Endowed with essentially the same genetic frailties, raised in the same environment, Rick made a conscious choice to rise above heredity and environment and fervently promised himself to walk a higher path than his parents. He consciously chose to refrain from alcohol and to develop the skills to nurture loving relationships.

Genetics and environment are *factors*. Admittedly, extremely influential ones. But, that's all they are. They are *only* factors, not *determinants*. The determinant—the decisive element—in the lives of Rick and Charles is the degree of their ownership. Rick takes full, uncompromising responsibility for his strengths and weaknesses, and thoughtfully, deliberately, chooses his behavior. Charles chooses to dodge responsibility and hide behind excuses.

> *Responsibility. n. A detachable burden easily shifted to the shoulders of God, Fate, Fortune, Luck or one's neighbor. In the days of astrology it was customary to unload it upon a star.*
>
> Ambrose Pierce, The Devil's Dictionary

A UNIVERSAL METAPHOR

The example of Rick and Charles serves as an apt metaphor for teams and organizations. Some take ownership and devote their energy with laser-like focus on achieving their goals. Others bog down in the quagmire of unproductive thought and communication habits.

Ownership is an invariable hallmark of every competent human being and of every thriving organization. Like all other worthy traits and competencies, ownership doesn't just happen, it must be sought for and cultivated through effort and exercise. This handbook is designed to accelerate your learning and assist you in putting the principles and practices of ownership into your daily life.

The consummate truth of life
we alter our destiny by altering our
The mind is our most crucial resource, ou
our ultimate arena of battl

THE GENESIS OF OWNERSHIP... AND OF NON-RESPONSIBILITY

Although dramatically different in their effects, both Ownership and Non-Responsibility flow from the same source—they are both products of the mind.

And, although they come from the same source, they do not occur and cannot exist in the same mind at the same time—they have to be exchanged for one another. *Each is a choice.*

Our thought processes make or break us.

Literally.

MOUNTING EVIDENCE

In our technologically advancing generation we have gained ways of studying ourselves that were unavailable to researchers even a few decades ago. We can now observe the brain in its actual states of operation. We can watch ourselves think and respond.

These studies confirm and expand truths that have been respected for quite some time. The value of positive thinking has been extolled for years, but in the 1990s science documented the literal biochemical reality of it. Biochemists discovered that a specific thought—chosen voluntarily in a human mind—is immediately translated into a molecular equivalent called a neurotransmitter (NTM), and these NTMs communicate with the cells, tissues, and systems of the body, telling them what to do and at what rate to do it. Remarkably, a specific thought generates a specific neurotransmitter which in turn exerts a specific impact on the physiology of the body.

Unfortunately, science gave these NTMs unwieldy names that don't mean much to the lay person. Dopamine, acetylcholine, serotonin, and melatonin are examples. It might have been more useful if science had selected names for the transmitters that relate to the states of mind that promote and perpetuate them. For instance, a lot of people go through life generating a fair amount of *Irritonin* in their systems. In women it could be called Frustrogen, and in men, Pistosterone.

The scenario works like this: We receive a memo or e-mail—someone changes our schedule or reaches a decision that impacts our momentum. Within milliseconds the vessels in our neck constrict, our complexion changes color, our blood pressure soars, and we're in a frank case of upset. And we think it's due to the memo, when in actuality these physical-emotional events have been triggered by our interpretative thoughts about the memo.

Levity aside, the important point to bear in mind is that, regardless of the names, the NTMs generated by thoughts both *affect* and *effect* our physiology. Our states of body at any given moment are a print-out of our states of mind. Directly and literally. If for no other reason than for the good of our health, it pays us to take control of our thoughts and to consider our perceptions and interpretations of events and experiences.

FUN AND FEAR AT THE FAIR

Picture a young couple about to take an amusement ride at a state fair. Up to this point, they've both been enjoying each other's company and the exhibits they've visited. Both in very positive moods, their respective body chemistry would tend to be similar and positive.

As they buckle into the seats of a high-speed thrill ride, however, their states of mind—and the resultant physical effects—become markedly dissimilar. While the woman begins to anticipate a fun experience, the man becomes apprehensive and he allows his thoughts to conjure scenarios of accidents and injury. "What if the car breaks loose? What if the seat belts don't hold?" From this point on, though the sharp turns and dives are identical, these two people will have entirely different experiences. The woman relishes the speed and sharp turns; her reaction to the whole experience is one of joy and exhilaration. Corresponding to her interpretation of "joy ride," her body's pharmacy produces chemicals that elevate the activity and performance of her immune system. As she exits the ride her body will be well on its way to a healthier, more disease-resistant state.

Her date, on the other hand, makes a completely different interpretation of the stimuli. He's frightened and unnerved by the same factors that exhilarate his girl friend, and his body's internal pharmacy directly reflects those perceptions. His blood stream will be flooded with "stress hormones" which depress the activity of his immune system, elevate his cholesterol and constrict his arteries.

Same evening, same ride, same factors, but diametrically different results.

"No two people see the external world in exactly the same way. To every separate person a thing is what he thinks it is—in other words, not a thing, but a think."

Penelope Fitzgerald
British Author

MINDING THE GAP

Between stimulus and response there lies a gap. When we don't maintain high levels of awareness or presence of mind there doesn't seem to be a gap. Stimulus appears to generate a set response in a seemingly automatic cause-and-effect equation. Yet, most of us sense that we're not just a bag of reflexive responses to outside stimuli. We *think*, and because we think we are able to select any number of responses to a given stimulus or situation. And, almost invariably, whenever we choose to choose our responses, things work out better—both in the short-term and the long run.

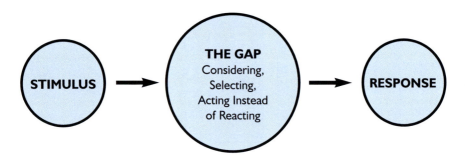

We enjoy notable breakthroughs and benefits when we "mind the gap" and take ownership of our mind's most amazing property—instantaneous self-analysis. Think of it! We can think about our thoughts, right in the process of thinking them, and can shift from one subject to another simply by willing to do so. Anytime we recognize that our thinking isn't constructive or useful, we can shift to something that is.

Hence, each of us is not only wholly responsible for his or her thoughts but for the effects that flow from them—our words, actions, habits, behavior—*and all the effects that flow from them.*

We're even responsible for the way we see the world and our experiences.

APPLICATION EXERCISE

EXERCISE A

Before proceeding, pause and think about the material you've just read. From the list below, please check two insights or concepts that have high value for you.

- ☐ Heredity is not the ultimate determinant in human behavior
- ☐ Ownership and non-responsibility are both mental creations
- ☐ We alter our destiny by altering our thoughts
- ☐ Thoughts translate into chemical messengers called neurotransmitters
- ☐ The state of the body is a direct reflection of the state of mind
- ☐ The "Gap Principle" – The ability to choose responses

What advantages, opportunities, or benefits do these insights afford you?

_____
_____
_____
_____
_____
_____
_____

In what ways will you apply those insights to real-life situations?

_____
_____
_____
_____
_____
_____
_____
_____

APPLICATION EXERCISE

EXERCISE B

Returning to the list, if there was a concept that you questioned, didn't totally agree with, or that you resisted, please check it (them) below.

- ☐ *Heredity is not the ultimate determinant in human behavior*
- ☐ *Ownership and non-responsibility are both mental creations*
- ☐ *We alter our destiny by altering our thoughts*
- ☐ *Thoughts translate into chemical messengers called neurotransmitters*
- ☐ *The state of the body is a direct reflection of the state of mind*
- ☐ *The "Gap Principle" – The ability to choose responses*

If you chose to set aside your reservations and accept the idea, what advantages or benefits could come to you? List them below.

_____
_____
_____
_____

If you chose to look for one additional advantage or benefit, what would it be?

_____
_____
_____
_____

PONDER POINT:

Day by day, minute by minute, we sit in the driver's seat, just as we did in this exercise, deciding what things we'll accept or despise, embrace or reject. Consciously or habitually, we make choice after choice, harvesting what we plant with each one. The fact that we can think about our postures, shift our positions, and reverse our points of view means we control the quantity and quality of our individual harvest, and underscores the immense value in elevating our consciousness and "minding the gap."

WHAT RECESSION?

We've all seen examples of people who've recognized opportunity amid adverse circumstances, seeing more than others could see at the time, and making the proverbial "lemonade out of lemons." One of the most successful car dealerships in the world moved into prominence during a so-called "recession" in the auto industry. Despite pessimistic forecasts, this dealership saw opportunity and chose to expand and aggressively pursue more business, while comparable dealerships chose to cut back and retrench. "We refuse to participate in the up-coming recession," became the company mantra, and they seized a substantial new chunk of market share during the supposed "bad times" and never looked back.

WHAT GOOD NEWS?

We also know people who can't seem to see the optimistic side of anything. They're so caught up in an unproductive mindset that they've mastered the ability to take good news and convert it into gloom.

> "Hey, Bob, did you see this? Management says they'll take us on a trip to Tahiti if we hit our goals this quarter."

> "Tahiti, eh. A total jungle. The mosquitoes are bigger than 747s. We'll all come back with malaria or something. Well, doesn't matter; those goals are a joke. We'll never hit 'em anyway."

While the foregoing quip is intended to put a smile on your face, the principle we're talking about is no laughing matter. In the most stinging irony of life, whether we see opportunity amid calamity or see calamity amid opportunity has little to do with the outward composition of events. Rather, it has everything to do with the inward composition of our selected point of view about the world.

A NAME FOR THE PRINCIPLE

At Quma Learning, we've given this principle a name. We call it **The Othello Principle**, derived from the tragedy, *Othello*, by William Shakespeare. Shakespeare's works still hang around in our literature classes and theatres because of the enduring relevance of their themes. No exception, Othello casts a light on the import and consequences of the timeless principle we're addressing.

Here's the plot: *Othello* is a Moor living in Venice. Though somewhat of an outsider, he is a respected military leader and war hero. The center of his life is his relationship with the beautiful Desdemona, who returns his love and is deeply committed to Othello in every way. Into this ideal scene enters, Iago, perhaps the most evil villain in Shakespearean writ. Through insinuation and implication, Iago plants ideas in Othello's mind, evoking suspicions about Desdemona's devotion and fidelity, implying that she is carrying on a love affair with another man. Before long, Othello becomes convinced that Iago, who he perceives to be a loyal friend, is right. Working himself into a fit of jealous rage, Othello murders his beloved wife, only to discover later that Iago is the betrayer, and that he (Othello) has destroyed the most beautiful thing in his life.

The crux of the Othello tragedy is that in actuality Desdemona was completely committed to Othello all along—faithful in every way. No glimmer of infidelity tainted her actions. But, Othello, *looking for* evidence of betrayal, *saw* in that very behavior sufficient evidence to convince himself of her deceit and duplicity.

Before you turn the page, see if you can put Shakespeare's point into a single sentence:

_____
_____
_____
_____

THE OTHELLO PRINCIPLE

The Eye Sees What the Mind Looks For

What timeless truth is conveyed in the Othello tragedy?
The Eye Sees What the Mind Looks For!

The eyes only gather data; it's the mind that gives it meaning. That's both the good news and the bad, because the principle can work for our good as well as our detriment. It's all in how we use it. Othello, unaware of the peril lurking within his own un-examined perceptions, fell prey to them. Despite Iago's evil role in the matter, ultimately Othello was his own worst enemy. He's the one who allowed his insecurities to billow into suspicions and then into hardened, rage-evoking conclusions. Othello saw faithlessness in the face of faithfulness *because he was looking for it*!

Here lies a lesson for us all. If we look for weaknesses and imperfections in our significant other, guess what we'll see? If we look for ways that our children or our co-workers don't perform their duties, guess what we'll see? If we look for hypocrisy or incompetence in upper level management, guess what we'll see? In every memo, every meeting, every policy change or new initiative, we'll sit back in our cynical chair and start collecting and cataloging the atrocities.

The Othello Principle aligns with enduring wisdom from the Talmud:

*We do not see things as they are,
we see them as we are.*

*We do not hear things as they are,
we hear them as we are.*

In a striking form of "self-fulfilling prophecy," people see what they want to see, believe (and collect evidence to support) what they choose to believe, and find what they search for.

A few decades ago a barefoot lawyer became a potent spiritual and political force in the world. His family name was Gandhi, and his parents named him Mohandas. He came up with a means of creating social action and change that he called *Satyagraha* which advocated tolerance and nonviolence. To draw attention to his causes he gave a certain number of speeches, held a certain number of fasts, and made a certain number of marches. Some people saw those fasts and heard those speeches and concluded that his parents did not give him the right name. Instead of calling him Mohandas, they called him Mahatma, which means "Great Soul."

Other people saw the same fasts and marches, listened to the same speeches, and watched the same events unfold and concluded that Gandhi wasn't fit to draw breath. One of these people, upset over Gandhi's tolerance for all creeds and religions, walked up to him, shoved a pistol into his stomach, and pulled the trigger.

One group of people looked for the good in the man and saw a Great Soul, and another group looked for the harms they thought he was doing to their culture and saw a threat.

Same speeches, same fasts, same marches, same soul. The difference was not in the "evidence" but the *interpretation* of the evidence. Each group saw what they looked for.

Be the change you wish to see in others.

Mahatma Gandhi

QUESTIONING OUR OWN AGENDAS

Although each of us tends to feel that our perceptions are perfect—accurate, unbiased observations of the truth about the world—and need no scrutiny, we must guard against locking into such a prideful position. As the lyrical words of Alexander Pope remind us,

> Of all the causes that conspire to blind
> Man's erring judgment, and misguide the mind,
> What the weak head with strongest bias rules,
> Is pride, the never-failing vice of fools.

A pertinent question to ask ourselves from time to time is "What am I looking for right now?" Clearly, some of our pre-conceived notions do not serve us, and we'll never see which ones they are unless we undertake a little self-assessment.

Shifting "what we're looking for" can have immediate and near revolutionary impact on all that we do. Even such routine events as meetings and conversations can be transformed within seconds. If, for example, Bob and Sally are having an argument—each certain that the other person is dead wrong and each needs to prove it to the other—no real communication will take place. They may call their exchange a dialogue but it's really just jousting monologues. Each will be "listening" combatively, concentrating on the next retort, looking for how best to thwart or deflect the other's points, rather than looking for points of agreement and ways to accommodate the other's needs.

> *My wife says I never listen to her...*
> *or something like that.*
>
> *Steven Wright*

If, however, instead of exchanging volleys with Sally, Bob chose to shift his "agenda" or "goal" in the conversation from *winning to understanding*, the whole tenor of the moment would instantly change. And, if they both shifted from finding holes in the other's arguments to finding areas of agreement, they'd save a small fortune in counseling bills and attorney's fees.

A communication expert I met said that the perception underlying every unsuccessful communication comes down to "I'm right, you're wrong, and I'll fight you for control." The moment a person lays that view aside, the sun breaks through the war clouds.

> I am just a poor boy.
> Though my story's seldom told,
> I have squandered my resistance
> For a pocketful of mumbles,
> Such are promises
> All lies and jest
> Still, a man hears what he wants to hear
> And disregards the rest.
>
> *The Boxer*
> song by Paul Simon, 1969

Perception is an invention—a construct of our own creation—not just affecting but *effecting* our experience in life. If we don't grasp and apply this insight, we get stuck in a certain set of perspectives and our progress becomes confined and constrained. When we couple that insight with the "Gap Principle"—the realization that we can consciously alter, elevate and improve our constructs any time we put our mind to it—we can be liberated and empowered by the Othello Principle.

Perception is a mirror not a fact. And what I look on is my state of mind, reflected outward.

A Course In Miracles
Course on Forgiveness Based on Christianity and Eastern Philosophy

APPLICATION EXERCISES FOR THE OTHELLO PRINCIPLE

Who am I?

The following exercise illustrates the point in a fun way. Each set of adjectives have been drawn from print and broadcast media sources in description of the same person. See if you can guess the identity:

1. Some people see me as…Disheveled, aloof, unteachable, reclusive, eccentric, and unattractive. Others see me as…Brilliant, unique, creative, unselfish, astute, and gifted.

   Who Am I?
   a) Ted Turner   b) Tom Peters   c) Albert Einstein   d) Howard Hughes

2. Some people see me as…Overly-protective, manipulative, superstitious, conniving, and arrogant. Others see me as…Caring, articulate, smart, diplomatic, elegant and refined.

   Who Am I?
   a) Rose Kennedy   b) Jackie Onassis   c) Barbara Bush   d) Nancy Reagan

3. Some people see me as…Pampered, over-rated, distant, lucky, unappreciative of my heritage, and self-absorbed. Others see me as…Approachable, personable, articulate, hard-working, dedicated, and a credit to my profession.

   Who Am I?
   a) Tiger Woods   b) Cher   c) Jane Fonda   d) John McEnroe

4. Some people see me as…Unfair, competitive to a fault, greedy, dishonest, self-serving, and dangerous. Others see me as…Energetic, entrepreneurial, visionary, philanthropic, brilliant, and principled.

   Who Am I?
   a) Bill Gates   b) Ralph Nader   c) Martha Stewart   d) Donald Trump.

5. Some people see me as...Insecure, fiendishly selfish, emotionally unstable, deceitful, immature and malicious. Others see me as...Charming, charitable, loving, over-flowing with class, and beautiful.

   Who Am I?
   a) Elizabeth Taylor b) Gwyneth Paltrow c) Princess Diana d) Diana Ross

6. Some people see me as...Untrustworthy, hypocritical, divisive, biased, pompous, and politically opportunistic. Others see me as...Charismatic, loyal, eloquent, spiritually guided, inspiring, and a leader in social consciousness.

   Who Am I?
   a) Jesse Jackson b) Pat Buchanan c) Pat Robertson d) Laura Schlesinger

7. Some people see me as a...Trouble-maker, rebel, felon, danger to order and society, disruptive, and evil. Others see me as a...Patriot, courageous reformer, peace-maker, visionary, and an icon of principled, selfless, tireless leadership.

   Who Am I?
   a) Nicholai Lenin b) Nelson Mandela c) Fidel Castro d) Martin Luther

Answers: 1) c 2) d 3) a 4) a 5) c 6) a 7) b

Real World Examples

"...the only thing we have to fear is fear itself."

Franklin Delano Roosevelt
32nd President of the United States of America

Samuel Johnson once said, "Depend on it, sir, when a man knows he is to be hanged in a fortnight, it concentrates his mind wonderfully." Unfortunately, Johnson's observation doesn't hold true in all cases. Sometimes the extreme pressure of "life or death situations" does not promote deep focus and concentration, but leads instead to panic, distraction, rattled emotions, and unraveled thinking as people become paralyzed with fear and doom. Once again it depends on the mental discipline and how people apply the Othello principle.

TO SUCCEED OR SURRENDER

During World War II, a tail gunner, Lyle Grant survived the crash of his B-17 when it was shot down over Nazi Germany, but was captured and imprisoned in a POW camp. As he and other prisoners were "oriented" to the bleak realities of their situation, they were told by their captors that virtually no means of escape existed—that their chances of success were less than ten thousand to one. Lyle thought, "Well, I'll take those odds," and he began to ponder and work out a plan, looking for ways and means of "beating the odds." As some of his fellow inmates got wind of his intentions, they tried to discourage him. Convinced in their own minds that escape was impossible, all they could see were "insurmountable obstacles" and they listed them, hoping to cure Lyle of his foolishness. Their eye saw what their mind looked for, and they were convinced thereby to just "face the facts," accept the situation, and hope that the allies would soon arrive to liberate them.

Lyle Grant was not dissuaded. He kept his mind riveted on his goal, and over time ideas came to him. Getting out of the camp was one thing, getting across enemy territory was another, and he planned and prepared accordingly. Piece by piece, various tools and necessities "coincidentally" fell into his hands, and eventually he had what he needed and he made his escape. After enduring withering adversities and deprivations, he successfully made his way across the lines to freedom.

This man relates his story in solemnity, thanking God for his life, because many of his fellow prisoners didn't make it home. Many of those who resigned themselves to the "impossibility" of escape perished on a death march inflicted upon them by their captors as the advancing allies closed in on the failing Nazi resistance.

In this case, the point of focus was literally a matter of life and death. One prisoner saw possibility, looked for opportunities, and took action. Others saw impossibility, gave up, and literally became victims of the circumstances.

ANOTHER CASE OF LIFE OR DEATH

Lyle Grant's story of life and death bears resemblance to the experience of one of Quma Learning's clients. The Cellular Infrastructure Group of a well-known electronics manufacturer was under fire. Product quality had sagged, customer complaints were rising, and they were getting drubbed by their competition. Rumors began flying around the company that upper level management was seriously considering either shutting the group down or selling them off.

The group leader recognized that ultimately the biggest threat to the group was the distraction and inaction that were setting in due to disproportionate focus on being laid off or sold. So *he* took action and rallied his colleagues and co-workers around the principles and methods of *The Ownership Spirit*.

Shifting their focus from "dread and fear" to finding solutions to the real issues, the majority of the team committed to *create* rather than *react*, and "play the game to win, rather than not to lose." They kicked their thinking into higher gears and challenged themselves to elevate quality, regain market share, and prove their worth. As they picked up the pace, a feeling of excitement and confidence began to pervade the group and momentum grew. Not surprisingly, they not only saved the division and produced huge chunks of profit, but they actually overachieved on their defect reduction goal. They ended up tripling their targeted improvement.

"No matter what problem you may have to face today, there is a solution, because you have nothing to deal with but your own thoughts.

As you know, you have the power to select and control your thoughts, difficult though it may be at times to do so. As long as you think that your destiny is in the hands of other people, the situation is hopeless."

Remind yourself constantly that you have nothing to deal with but your own thoughts. Write it down where you can see it often. Have it on your desk. Hang it in your bathroom. Write it in your pocketbook. Write it on your soul. It will transform your life.

Emmet Fox
American Author

Self-Diagnosis and Self-Improvement

"Success on any major scale requires you to accept responsibility…In the final analysis, the one quality that all successful people have is the ability to take on responsibility."

Michael Korda
Editor-in-Chief, Simon & Schuster

SELF-DIAGNOSIS

Despite the fact that we've all heard, "Perception is reality," few of us stop to really ponder the implications. Fewer still ever *use* that insight as a tool for improvement, especially when it comes to self-improvement.

Most of us seem to possess a sharp eye for recognizing the self-inflicted snares and mental booby traps that others create for themselves, but experience utter blindness when it comes to our own. Part of the reason for this myopia is that our thoughts are so much a part of us and come so naturally and seemingly automatically that it takes considerable "presence of mind" to step back and analyze our thoughts objectively.

Now that we see the significance and implications of the Othello Principle, we need to work on and build our self-awareness so that we can tap into the huge potential that it offers.

ANALYZE THE FOLLOWING

Visualizing the following scenarios, briefly develop a likely sequence of thoughts and the results that flow from them for each scenario, as in the following example:

Example Scenario: Your boss retired and has been replaced by someone within the ranks, rather than yourself or someone from the outside.

Position A:
I deserved this opportunity a lot more than he/she.

I can't believe the politics everybody plays around here. It's not what you do or how hard you work that counts, it's who you can "brown nose." It's so unfair! This place stinks.

What results will flow from this line of thinking?

Promotes distrust, disunity, resentment, hostility, resignation and, on the personal level, a whole truckload of unhealthy physical consequences.

Position B:
I'm going to support him/her like I'd like to be supported.

I'm disappointed, yes, but I'm going to look past that and get behind this person. If we work as a team, my strengths can blend with his/hers and maybe we'll both learn something in the process. I'm sure as heck not going to let this ruin my life.

What results will flow from this line of thinking?

Unity, teamwork, enthusiasm for the job, higher productivity—individually and collectively. And, perhaps most importantly, peace.

SCENARIO ONE

Your boss retired and has been replaced with a hire from the outside, rather than from within the ranks of the company.

Position A:
A fresh perspective might be just what we need.

_____

_____

_____

What results will flow from this line of thinking?

_____

_____

_____

_____

Position B:
This person has no idea what's going on here.

_____

_____

_____

What results will flow from this line of thinking?

_____

_____

_____

_____

SCENARIO TWO

In a planning session, several of your ideas are not given consideration.

Position A:
I'm not a creative person. My ideas are duds.

_____
_____
_____
_____

What results will flow from this line of thinking?

_____
_____
_____
_____

Position B:
I have a high batting average for good ideas.

_____
_____
_____
_____

What results will flow from this line of thinking?

_____
_____
_____
_____

SCENARIO THREE

Despite your clear communication of the expectations and the consequences, your son still doesn't keep his bedroom clean.

Position A:
I never get any respect. He's taking advantage.

_____
_____
_____

What results will flow from this line of thinking?

_____
_____
_____
_____

Position B:
I know he loves and respects me.

_____
_____
_____

What results will flow from this line of thinking?

_____
_____
_____
_____

SCENARIO FOUR

One of your direct reports fails to follow through on an assignment, despite a thorough explanation of its importance and discussion of what was expected.

Position A:
I can't count on this person. I wonder if he has the ability to do this job.

_____

_____

_____

What results will flow from this line of thinking?

_____

_____

_____

_____

Position B:
This person is competent and capable and has come through on assignments in the past.

_____

_____

_____

What results will flow from this line of thinking?

_____

_____

_____

_____

The Assessor

"It takes a painful reassessment...to see how much of our ineffectiveness is caused by ourselves. In you lie both the major causes and the major solutions of your problems with wasted time."

R. Alec Mackenzie
American Author

WHAT DID IT LOOK LIKE TO YOU?

At this point, how have you chosen to look at the previous exercises? Did you see them as a superficial chore or a real opportunity to learn the material in greater depth? Did you simply scan the scenarios, getting the idea without really doing the work? Did you forego the effort, thinking that you "already know this stuff" rather than giving a full measure of effort to increase your skills?

Can you see the real and practical implications of The Othello Principle? Can you see how universal it is? What each of us looks for, even in terms of this book, directly impacts how much each will get out of any experience. Some readers will *look for* ways of getting the most out of the material, others will just skim the surface. Some people will genuinely strive to improve, others will just seek confirmation that they're "already there," and this stuff applies to somebody else.

In every experience, The Othello Principle applies. We see what we look for, setting the thermostat for how much value we gain, add, or forfeit in every situation. And, we live with those decisions for better or for worse, constantly.

A TOOL, NOT JUST AN EXERCISE

Let's formalize these concepts into a concrete method of shifting our thinking into more productive gears. We call this tool **"The Assessor"** for two reasons: First, it helps us slow down and *assess* our thinking, examine our perceptions and explore multiple ways of looking at a given situation. Second, the word "assessor" serves as a functional acronym to keep the steps in mind.

THE ASSESSOR

A - Accept. *Accept* the idea that taking a moment to contemplate any given situation can save time and improve results in the long run. Also, *accept* the idea that no matter how effective we are, we can always improve, and that we'll never elevate our performance until we elevate our thinking.

S - State. In writing, *state* how you see the scenario at this point. If you have a definite energy about the situation, be it confidence, irritation, resignation, or whatever, jot it down. Then describe why. Dump out the whole bucket, expressing feelings as well as thoughts in your description.

S – Suppose. Once you've captured your current outlook, take a dispassionate, analytical approach by *suspecting* that you may not have all the facts or the entire picture. Make yourself *suppose* for a moment that you're not totally accurate—that your information is incomplete. You might even entertain the *supposition* that you're dead wrong about the whole situation.

E – Explore. Explore two or three different scenarios, pursuing the course of thoughts flowing from each supposition just as you did in the previous exercise. See if those shifts might not produce more favorable outcomes and open up greater possibilities. Visualize each scenario in some detail.

S – Select. After due consideration, select the best option.

S – Shift. Put the option into the practice. Create an action plan in your mind or on paper, and then implement it. Visualize the behavior that would flow from your newly chosen premise, including the benefits. Set up a few reminders to help keep your awareness active.

O – Observe. As you move forward, stay alert. Keep in mind, "By their fruits ye shall know them." If you start seeing improved responses from other people and/or better results from your efforts, you'll know you're on a better plane. If not, go back to the beginning of The Assessor and try again.

R – Retain. When golfers hit a good shot, they're advised to pause and repeat "the mental movie" of their shot in their mind before they move on. By mental repetition they reinforce positive images and accelerate progress. Apply the same principle here. Many people find that journaling is an excellent way of reinforcing successes, allowing them to review and rehearse it from time to time in the future.

A PROBLEM WITH TIE BREAKERS

A case study from the files of Dr. James Loehr, sports psychologist, parallels perfectly the steps in The Assessor and illustrates the effect.

Several years ago, when Tom Gullickson played team tennis for Phoenix, he developed a pattern of losing close matches. In particular, he seldom won any set that wound up in a tie breaker, his success rate falling far below the law of averages. "I hate it when I get to tie breakers," he often muttered out loud without recognizing that statement for its diagnostic value.

Finally, his frustration led him to suspect that something more than luck or coincidence was at work. Employing Dr. Loehr as a coach, he explained, "I need help. I lose so many important matches in tie breakers. I hate 'em." Loehr quickly saw what Gullickson did not (at first), and made Tom agree to try something. "I want you to say out loud, 'I love tie breakers' twenty-five times a day. Write it on a card, put it on the mirror.

At first Gullickson was skeptical but, somewhat reluctantly, he complied. A few weeks later he called his coach. "I won a tie breaker, but I'm not ready to believe it was due to the self-talk," he said. "Have you been doing it?" "Yes, but I'm not convinced that this isn't just coincidence."

A short time later, Tom won a match that included two tie breakers both of which he had won. Shortly after that, Tom found himself in a very important match with his arch nemesis, John Alexander. Alexander won the first two sets, but during the third set Gullickson noticed himself thinking, "If I can just get this guy to a tie breaker, I can beat him." He did and he won the third set, and then the fourth. In the fifth and final set, it was close all the way, and as time went on Gullickson became ever more confident. He felt like the match was playing right into his strength. The set eventuated into a tie breaker and Gullickson defeated Alexander.

THE ASSESSOR EXEMPLIFIED

Gullickson's experience parallels the eight-step progression of our self-assessment tool, The Assessor. Note the following:

Accept: Gullickson accepted the idea that something more than coincidence was at work and that he might be the central factor. Much like Pogo's quip, "We have met the enemy, and he is us."

State: He had no trouble fulfilling this step. He'd been repeating this self-defeating statement hundreds of times in his mind, which is often the case with all of us.

Suppose: Tom's coach got him to suspect that his repeated expression (thought) of detesting tie breakers was actually the crux of the issue.

Explore: In this case the remedy is so straight-forward that entertaining multiple scenarios wasn't even necessary. Loehr cut right to the "chase scene" with a direct approach to shifting Gullickson's inner (and frequently outer) dialogue.

Select: The choice was obvious—reverse the verb "hate" to "love." And, this is true of so many of our own self-inflicted obstacles. They are not really all that complex when we get right down to them.

Shift: The shift was accomplished just as we described a few pages back. Loehr had Gullickson not only rehearse the stronger thought regularly, but he urged him to set up reminders so that he wouldn't drop back into his "default mode."

Observe: The results spoke for themselves. When Gullickson began looking with confidence at the subject of tie breakers, guess what he saw? And, not surprisingly, that's what he got.

Retain: Gullickson drew on his recent past successes in tie breakers when it came down to "crunch time" in his match with Alexander. And, the mental images and reinforcement that he gained from that victory galvanized his confidence for months to come.

APPLYING THE OTHELLO PRINCIPLE

Hone your skill in applying The Othello Principle by completing the following:

APPLICATION

In connection with the September 11, 2001, attack on America, many heroic deeds were published. In the space below, please list two or three examples of the Ownership Spirit that stand out in your memory.

_____
_____
_____
_____

Even amid great tragedy, people are able to identify positives that flow out of such events when they look for them. Looking back on the changes that have taken place, in the space below, list some of the positives that you see.

_____
_____
_____

Considering the events in the past few months, is your view of the future more optimistic or less optimistic than it was in late September 2001?

_____
_____
_____

Are you aware that by making a conscious decision to do so, you could reverse the opinion you just stated above and find evidence to support your reversal? Try it. Think of an example or a reason to support the opposite opinion and write it below. If you think about it long enough, in fact, you can probably come up with several.

_____
_____
_____
_____
_____

THE UPSIDE

Clearly, the shifting of underlying assumptions has marked impact on our opinions and our very experience of life itself. Realizing that we have the innate ability to weigh our assumptions, evaluate them, and make choices to continue or curtail them, affords each of us a sobering combination of power, freedom, responsibility and accountability.

We urge you to give that a great deal of thought.

"We have only one person to blame, and that's each other"

Larry Breck
NHL Hockey Player

*"Sometimes I get the feeling
that the whole world is
against me, but deep down
I know that's not true.
Some of the smaller
countries are neutral."*

Robert Orben

The Owner/Victim Choice

Transforming Victim Thinking
One Thought at a Time

The Owner/Victim Choice Objective

Define and understand the thinking and language patterns of Owners and Victims

Distinguish and study specific contrasts in Owner-Thinking and Victim-Thinking

Apply insights from the contrasts to specific areas of personal behavior

Recognize personal self-victimization language habits

Employ a three-step method of transforming unproductive patterns to productive ones

Increase personal application of the Ownership Spirit

The Owner/Victim Choice

Transforming Victim Thinking One Thought at a Time

Table of Contents

52	The Owner/Victim Choice Objectives
55	Definitions
55	Recommendations
57	Self-Recognition Exercise
59	Emphasizing Application

OWNER/VICTIM CONTRASTS

61	Independent/Dependent
69	Live by choice/Live against their will
73	Get from/Get through
79	Higher purpose/Lower purpose
85	Seldom take offense/Easily offended
89	Use life/Used by life
95	Take responsibility/Shift responsibility
99	The programmer/The program
106	Transforming Victim Habits
108	Recommendations for Increased Ownership
110	Owner/Victim Worksheet

*In life, there are Owners
and there are Victims.*

In life there are Owners and there are Victims.

In this handbook, we won't use those terms as glib labels to throw on people, but as descriptions of two ways of approaching any situation—two ways of going about our jobs and our careers— two ways of living life.

DEFINITIONS

When we refer to Owners, we're not talking about people who hold legal control or majority stock in a company or business. We're referring to a powerful, productive state of mind, where we take both responsibility and initiative for personal and team success. When we behave like Owners, we bring high levels of commitment and energy to everything we do. We see ourselves being more powerful than circumstances and able to impact change wherever we go, acting rather than reacting, being more of a cause than an effect.

When we refer to Victims, we're not talking about people who have suffered real injustice or abuse due to the acts of others, or who've been literally injured through no fault of their own. Again, we're referring to a state of mind. When we're stuck in Victim-thinking, we see the course of events as a series of negative incidents happening to us. We become demoralized and ineffective because we perceive that we're being acted upon by unfriendly forces beyond our control (sometimes called "the boss" or "the company"). Without realizing it, we discount our ability to make a difference, resulting in an overall sense of helplessness, resignation and anger.

Victim-thinking acts like a governor on the mental throttle, stifling productivity and squandering talents. Owner-thinking leads to high energy, greater accomplishment, deeper satisfaction, and dramatically improved results.

RECOMMENDATIONS

No matter where we might be on the Owner/Victim scale, we can sharpen our edge. To do so, remember three things:

First: Keep thinking in terms of patterns, not people.

Although we'll speak of Owners and Victims as though they were separate identities, we're actually talking about two patterns of thought and behavior, not "types" of people.

In actuality, there's a bit of victim in all of us. No one is, at all times and in all places, a perfect owner. Neither are any of us complete victims. Our behavior is a composite of both patterns; sometimes we behave like owners and sometimes we don't. We accrue big rewards when we elevate awareness of our own thinking tendencies. We can recognize when we're running unproductive mental software and replace it with more productive trains of thought.

Second: Listen to your own language.

Thought and language go hand in hand. Thinking is the mind's way of communicating with itself. As you read these pages, your conscious mind is framing ideas by using sentences and paragraphs as your means of inner expression. And, when we want to understand what *someone else* is thinking, we ask them questions, gaining insights into their thinking by analyzing the tone and words of their response.

Thus, one of the best diagnostic tools to distinguish Victim-thinking from Owner-thinking is to notice language. The words of the mouth reveal the thought patterns of the mind.

> "To be conscious that we are perceiving or thinking is to be conscious of our own existence."
> — *Aristotle*

Third: Amplify the positive, reprogram the negative.

Unfortunately, many of us go through life with a fairly low level of thought awareness. We seldom pause to think about our thinking and challenge ourselves to look for better approaches. As a consequence, we get stuck in unproductive patterns—mental ruts—primarily because we don't recognize the pattern or rut for what it is—a choice.

The diagnostic tool on the next two pages will help you increase your ability to recognize the thinking patterns of both Owners and Victims. If you are really bold, you may invite friends or family to offer their perceptions of your thought and language patterns. Comparing the results can offer valuable insight! Effective trains of thought can be celebrated, emphasized, and repeated, while counterproductive patterns can be discarded or reprogrammed. The combination of amplifying what works and redesigning what doesn't, leads to whole new levels of personal effectiveness.

SELF-RECOGNITION EXERCISE

Do any of the statements on the following pages sound familiar, even if these may not be your exact words? Place a check in the column that best reflects the frequency of occurrence of these Owner and Victim statements in your own thinking.

Victim Statement	Frequency		
	often	sometimes	seldom
I know more than (he/she) does. Why do I have to listen to this?			
If I just had some help on this.			
If I hear the term "paradigm shift" one more time I'll scream.			
I wish things were different.			
Give it a few days. Let's see if they're really serious about all this.			
I can't help it. I've always been the type of person who…			
I'll be glad when I'm finished with this rat race.			
Don't ask me. I'm only the…			
No good deed ever goes unpunished.			
I wish they'd give me more meaningful work.			
I can't do one more thing. I'm swamped.			
When is management going to wake up and fix this?			
Never pays to get your hopes up.			
I'm no dreamer, I gotta be real. I'm no phony.			
They never give us the resources to do the job.			
Just my luck.			
My (teammates, family) never take any initiative.			
That's just the way I am.			
Another initiative? What flavor is it this month?			
I don't know how they expect us to work under these conditions.			
My (boss, team members, spouse, family) doesn't/don't care what's happening to me.			
I can't wait until this over.			
I'll manage somehow.			
It drives me crazy when…			
I am just not a detail person.			
I can't believe he/she said that about me.			
What's the use? Nobody ever notices what I do.			
What do you expect? The market is soft.			
Why can't they figure it out?			
If they don't care, why should I?			

Owner Statement	Frequency		
	often	sometimes	seldom
If enough of us get behind this, we can make it work.			
I'm not going to let (him/her/them/it) spoil my day.			
How can I use this?			
In the future, I'm going to be more careful to…			
I've got an idea about what we can do to improve…			
I'm willing to give (this idea, this initiative) a chance.			
Let's make the most of these next few weeks.			
I see your point.			
Failure is not an option.			
Let's look at other ways to get it done.			
I need to provide more leadership in this situation.			
Count me in.			
We can look at it like it's a problem or we can seize an opportunity.			
How could we have some fun with this?			
How can I be more responsive to (my spouse, team, customers)?			
My team could help with that.			
What can I learn from this?			
Great idea. Thanks for the input.			
My current goal is to…			
I'm committed to accomplishing…			
I see it differently. Help me understand what you're saying.			
I'm fortunate because…			
No obstacle can withstand our sustained thinking and effort.			
You're right, I was wrong on that.			
It wasn't pleasant, but I learned a lot from that experience.			
How can I contribute?			
Our team will take that one on.			
I'm not in the best of moods right now. I'm put out with…			
Where do we want to go from here?			
I've got to communicate more clearly.			
What are our best options at this point?			
What can I do to help?			
I will…			
It didn't turn out like we wanted, but we can still…			
I apologize.			

EMPHASIZING APPLICATION

Our focus in this handbook is on application and results. We want to help you translate knowledge into productive behavior.

> *"O would some power the gift to give us to see ourselves as others see us!"*
>
> Robert Burns, Scottish poet

As you proceed through the contrasts in Owner/Victim thinking (language), you will see illustrations of both forms of expression, and will have opportunity to identify additional examples from your own life. We encourage you to record these examples on the worksheet provided on pages 110 and 111 of this handbook. As you complete each section, turn to the worksheet and write down examples that are meaningful to you. Then take a moment to think about recent experiences in your life. Jot down examples of both owner and victim language that you recall from your conversations and interactions with others —both things that you've thought and said, as well as what others have said.

Making a list of owner and victim statements will accomplish three purposes: It will (1) sharpen your focus as you read the material, heightening memory and recall, (2) elevate awareness of your current language habits, helping you be more selective, and (3) accelerate the depth and the speed of your behavior change.

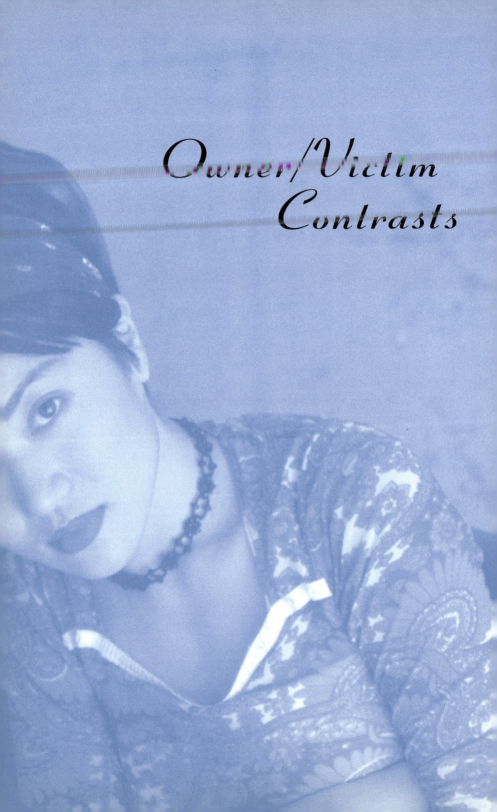
Owner/Victim Contrasts

Independent/Dependent

Owners live independent of circumstance.

They choose their moods, attitudes, and states of being. Their inner world is not just a reflex response to the outer world.

A Victim's inner world is almost always a direct reflection of the outer world. Victims are highly dependent on circumstantial input.

When Victims receive a compliment, they're up; when they receive a word of criticism, they're down. Emotionally, they're like corks bobbing on the ocean, driven by the shifting winds of circumstance.

Put more clearly, Victims think they need a reason to be happy. If an Owner comes into work with a bounce in the step, a smile on the face, humming a tune, a Victim is likely to ask, "What's made you so happy?"

Behind the Victim's question lies an assumption that happiness is a by-product of some outside entity or occurrence.

"What happened to you today? Did you win the lottery or something?"

A sarcastic Victim may even ask "What's wrong with you?" suggesting that happiness is an abnormality.

If the Owner responds with "Oh, nothing really, I'm just happy," the Victim will think that's weird—that something's wrong with the Owner.

"You mean you're happy for no reason?"
"Yes, I've just decided to be happy today."
"Whoa. That's strange. Real strange. Have you seen a counselor about this?"

Like Victims, Owners have their share of adversity, but they don't let that drive their mood or behavior. They realize they can be pleasant and positive despite adverse circumstances. They know that emotional states are a decision, not some overpowering sentiment imposed upon them by some outside force that they're unable to resist. They know that people decide to be up or decide to be down. And, since they see it as a choice and that choosing to be up produces better results, they opt for the approach that offers the best outcomes.

TO ACT-AND-ADVANCE OR WAIT-AND-WATCH

Since Victims believe that happiness and productivity are up to someone or something else, they spend a lot of time waiting for things to change. They expect somebody else to take the initiative. This tactic is very appealing because it's so safe. If things don't work out, the Victim can always gripe and say that they'd have done things differently.

> *"We'd better hold off until someone on a higher level
> takes a position on this."*

> *"Why doesn't leadership lead? They always leave us in the dark.
> I never know what they want me to do."*

Victims get trapped in hesitancy, allowing fear to bar them from stepping out or stepping up. They like to think that they're "movers and shakers," but mostly they're just shakers.

Many Victims drift into cynicism, and they adopt a "you'll-have-to-prove-it-to-me-first" attitude. Whenever management identifies a new initiative, Victims sit back and sneer, dumping doubt on the fires of change.

> *"Oh, great, here's another one. How long is this initiative going to last?
> Six weeks? Give it a month, it'll blow over. I'm not going to bust
> my butt until they've proven to me that they're serious.
> I'll give it …about eight years. Then, if they show me that
> they're really committed, I'll jump right in."*

An Owner wouldn't take that approach. An Owner would say:
> "We can't compete effectively if we're not willing to change.
> I'm going to get behind this initiative, right from the 'get-go.'
> If enough of us support it, we can make it work."

FOND OF THE FUTURE

Victims are frustrated people. They find the present an intolerable place and grow very fond of the future. You can hear it in their expressions. They talk about the future with an enormous longing, verbalizing the belief that the future will fix everything. Have you heard something like this before?

> *I'm so sick of high school and people telling me what to do.
> I can't wait to get to college and be on my own.*

> *Man, I'll be glad when this semester's over. I hate the pressure
> of making grades—these professors control my life.*

> *College life is getting old—real old. I'll sure be happy to get out into
> the real world and make some money.*

*Being "low person on the pecking order" isn't my idea of a challenging career.
Most of this stuff they have me do is beneath my education anyway.
I just wished they'd give me something really challenging to do.*

*Why does everything get dumped on me? I am swamped.
Where's all the help they keep promising me.*

*I'll be glad when these ridiculous deadlines pass. Don't they think
I have a life? I would love to finally see one of my kid's ball games.*

*Nobody appreciates what I do. I'm working like a dog to make
somebody else rich. I ought to start my own business someday.*

*Making payroll every two weeks is tough.
Nobody knows the pressure I'm under.
I wish somebody would come along and buy me out.
I can't wait for retirement. No more pressure, no more
complaining customers and whining employees.*

*My back's killing me, I wish the doctor could figure out what's wrong.
It would sure be great to be young again. Ah, high school—those were the days!*

Victims can hardly wait to get out of the present. It's not a happy place for them, and they cling to the vain hope that the future will fix what's bothering them. They want to *escape* to the future.

This brings up the question, "What's wrong with looking forward to the future? Don't Owners look forward to the future?" The answer, of course, is "Yes." Owners definitely look forward to the future, but they view the future much differently than Victims. They look forward to it while experiencing substantial joy in the journey. They're reasonably content with the present, and they expect even better things ahead because they are designing them.

*"Your success and happiness lie in you.
External conditions are the accidents of life"*

Helen Keller

APPLICATION

Pause for a moment and think about the section you've just read. On the application page (pages 110-111), write down two Victim statements and two Owner statements based on the contrasts just described.

EXAMPLES

Victim Language	Owner Language
My boss can be such a jerk sometimes. She makes me so mad!	I'm not going to let my boss's idiosyncrasies bother me so much. I'm going to enjoy what I do and get on with it.
Mondays are a pain. I get depressed just thinking about them.	There are at least two things I want to accomplish this Monday. Specifically, they are…
I hate planning anything with the Andersons. They're always late.	When we plan something with the Andersons, let's allow a few extra minutes and just slow down and enjoy it.
You spent how much on that pair of shoes?	Honey, Quma Learning has a great course on money management. Would you like to go with me?

"We build our future, thought by thought, for good or ill, yet know it not."

Henry Van Dyke

PONDER POINTS
Independent vs. Dependent

How do my moods impact my performance? How do they impact other people? Do I *choose* my moods?

Do I explore and embrace new initiatives? How do I approach change: Am I willing to expend real effort in trying something new or do I have a "wait-and-watch" mentality? Think of a recent personal experience that supports your answer.

How do I approach the present? Do I make the most of current opportunities, or do I often feel trapped by circumstances?

How do I approach the future? Do I see how the present helps create my future? Am I excited about what the future will bring, or do I long to get out of my current situation? Am I expecting the future to make the changes, or am I making them?

FOCAL POINT
What one thing will I do to live more independent of circumstance?

_____
_____
_____
_____
_____
_____
_____
_____
_____
_____

Live by choice/Live against their will

Owners see life as a precious gift and an opportunity—
something to be savored, appreciated, and used to the fullest.
In their conversation you'll hear phrases like:

"I'm trying something new, and
I'm excited about the possibilities."

"Currently, my goal is to…"

"I'm working toward…"

"I'm fortunate because…"

"I'm choosing to…"

Owners talk about where they're going and what they're enjoying. They're appreciative of opportunity. Anyone who has experienced the "fragility of life" seldom takes life for granted. Owners would never describe life as a drudgery or some kind of punishment.

A Victim's bumper sticker states, "The more you complain, the longer God makes you live." Such sardonic humor veils a prevalent Victim attitude— *Victims seem to live life against their will.*

Nothing ever seems voluntary to a Victim. They act like they are being forced into every breath they take. Without realizing it, Victims labor under the tyranny of self-imposed constraint.

"Look at my desk. What a mess. Looks like I'll have to clean it up."

"I have to go to work. Do you think I asked for all these responsibilities?

*Where did all these kids come from anyway?
I didn't ask for these children; they're my spouse's idea."*

Another characteristic of individuals who live life against their will is the vilifying of *They.* Victims get this negative *they* going in their language. This ever-present, ever-evil group seems to be engaged in a purposeful, methodical conspiracy to make the Victim's life as miserable as diabolically possible. Whenever something goes wrong, Victims immediately know who's at fault — all those *"they's"* out there lurking in the bushes.

"They never listen to us."

"They have no idea what we're up against in this department."

*"If they weren't such victims, I wouldn't have
such a hard time being an owner."*

Owners live life out of choice, not constraint. Consequently, they have increased energy and joy, and they accomplish a great deal more.

PONDER POINTS
Live by choice/Live against their will

Do others perceive me as a grateful person?

Do I take time during the day to notice how interesting, even amazing, the world is?

What good cause or effort do I support?

Do I frequently feel forced to do things against my will?

Am I quick to whine or lay blame on others?

Do I often feel like I have few options in my life?

Do I express appreciation to others frequently or rarely?

Do I smile much?

FOCAL POINT
What one thing will I do to live life more by choice?

_____
_____
_____
_____
_____
_____
_____
_____
_____
_____

Owners have a "get from" attitude

Get from/Get through

Owners have a "get from" attitude—in the best sense of the term, or more clearly, a "learn from" attitude.

When Owners face difficulty, they ask themselves, "What can I learn from this? What can I take away from this that will make me a better person?" To Owners, trials are not unfair punishments, they're learning experiences.

Here is an example of an Owner describing a difficult time:

> "We had a family member enter a 12-step recovery program for an addiction. It wasn't very pleasant. I wouldn't want to face that again, but we got a lot from it. It wasn't easy, but we learned to communicate as a family. We learned how to support one another without being permissive. It was tough, but it turned out to be a valuable chapter. We learned the value of "tough love" and how to be honest with each other. I certainly didn't enjoy it, but I know we're all better off for having had this experience."

You can consider yourself on the graduate level of this trait when you can take this line of thinking one step further: What can I contribute?

We take big strides in Ownership when we think in terms of contribution instead of compensation. Owners find that career satisfaction comes from the same source as a successful marriage: A "How-Much-Can-I-Contribute" attitude, emphasizing the giving more than the receiving. People who enter marriages with the idea that the other person's role is to make them happy are consulting with lawyers in short order.

The same thing applies to a fulfilling career. If you go to work every day with the thought, "How much can I contribute?" you will have more than a prosperous career, you'll have a *fulfilling* career.

> "They laughed at Joan of Arc, but she went ahead and built it anyway."
>
> *Gracie Allen*

By contrast, Victims "get through" things—like projects and meetings.

> "O brother, how long is this one going to last? I'll bet this is going to be a big waste of time. What a pain, but (heavy sigh) I'll get through it."

Victims see every change as something to get through—like the conversion to a new computer system, or a new corporate initiative. They seldom see change as opportunity—something to embrace and enjoy. To them, nothing "new" is ever fun. It's always bad news—a painful odyssey that they have to endure.

Victims express themselves in the tone of a "heroic martyr." Like, "Hey, don't worry about me. It's something I shouldn't have to put up with, but I'll get through it." They talk about events as though they were calamities to overcome.

O: "How are things going at the company these days?"

V: "Well, we're scrambling to keep up. I've never had so much stress in all my life. Don't know if I'll get through it or not."

O: "How are things going with the kids?"

V: "Well, we've got teenagers. You know what that means. I'll sure be glad when we're through that stage."

O: "How are you and your significant other getting along?"

V: "Okay I guess. We're working through a few things. I think we'll make it."

O: "How are things going in your career?"

V: "Well, to be honest with you, I'll be glad when it's over. Yeah, I'm really looking forward to retirement. I'm kind of worried about death though, I've heard that's hard to get through."

APPLICATION

Pause for a moment and think about the section you've just read. On the application page (pages 110-111), write down two Victim statements and two Owner statements based on the contrasts just described.

EXAMPLES

Victim Language	Owner Language
Great, another meeting. I'll never get anything done if they keep making me go to all these stupid meetings.	What can we get accomplished today? How can I add value to this meeting?
Sorry, I can't make the meeting, Bob. I have to go out of town next week.	Please excuse me from the meeting, Bob. I'm planning to be in Boston next week.
My in-basket looks like Mt. Everest. Yuk, I guess I'll have to tackle that mess next week.	I'm going to get after this paper work. I don't want all that staring me in the face when I come to work on Monday.
I'll be glad when the rush is over. We're so busy, there's hardly time to grab a bite of lunch.	Business is booming! Thank Goodness.
I can't wait until I'm finished with night school. The load is doing me in.	It's hectic right now, but I'm learning a lot that's going to help my career.

PONDER POINTS
Get from/Get through

Do I frequently find myself learning great lessons from my experiences in life?

What actions in my life indicate my desire to make a difference?

Do I generate new possibilities in the face of challenge and adversity?

Which question do I ask more often, "What's in it for me?" or "How can I contribute?"

Do I make myself out to be a martyr and hope that others will sympathize with my difficult lot in life?

Do I view challenges as opportunities to grow or as burdens to carry?

FOCAL POINT
What will I do to get more from or contribute more to my current situation?

_____

_____

_____

_____

_____

_____

_____

_____

_____

_____

> *Higher purpose/Lower purpose*

Owners develop a sense of higher purpose.

They lift their sights and see the "big picture" in what they do. Although they're focused on doing their job, they see it as part of a mission or a valuable purpose.

THE MASON'S HELPERS

> A reporter saw a man carrying a load of bricks at a construction site and asked, "What's going on here, what are you doing?"
>
> "I'm carrying this load of bricks from that truck over there to this pile over here."
>
> The reporter replied, "Well, thanks for taking the time to answer my question." A few moments later the reporter saw another man carrying a similar load of bricks and asked, "What's going on here, what are you doing?"
>
> "I'm helping to build a great university. It's going to be a wonderful asset for our city, and maybe for all mankind. I was thinking that maybe the doctor who'll discover the cure for cancer will be educated right in this university. Engineers who'll create new technology to raise the world's standard of living may be trained here. It's going to be a great addition to our community, and I'm helping to build it."

Application of this principle is not limited to our professional pursuits. Think about your role and contribution to your family, friends, and community. Do you sense a higher purpose in your activities and endeavors, or do you diminish the part you play in these settings?

Every year during the holiday season a certain company encourages its employees to volunteer time to support a community relief organization. One employee described his experience as follows:

> "I'm just a bell ringer and I'm only here because my boss would chew me out if I didn't come. It's a little embarrassing standing in front of that store trying to get people to throw me their change, and besides, my ears ring for a week after I'm done."

Another person in the same company, volunteering at the same location described her experience this way:

> "Every year I look forward to spending some of my time during the holidays to raise money for people who need help. It warms my heart to think that families will have a good holiday meal and maybe a few presents because I'm willing to spend a couple of hours every year to help. I am always impressed with the generosity others show as they stop for a minute during their shopping to make a contribution. This service helps me feel the spirit of the holiday season."

Keep in mind that a "sense of higher purpose" is a creation. It's not something you find or buy. It's something you create and cultivate.

"Life is a mirror and will reflect back to the thinker what he thinks into it."

Ernest Holmes

APPLICATION

Pause for a moment and think about the section you've just read. On the application page (pages 110-111), write down two Victim statements and two Owner statements based on the contrasts just described.

EXAMPLES

Victim Language	Owner Language
I'm just the shuttle service. All I ever do is take kids places.	I'm glad my children have so many opportunities to develop their talents.
My friends always dump their problems on me.	It's good to know that my friends trust me enough to share the challenges they face.
What do you expect from me? I'm just the…	I need to learn more about what our customers expect of us.
Why do I need to have all this information about the customer? My job doesn't deal directly with them.	If we got a little creative here, I think we could surprise our customer with a little more…
It's not my job.	My team plays a key role in our overall business plan. We're directly responsible for…

PONDER POINTS
Higher purpose/Lower purpose

How does my daily performance promote the success of my company, my family, and my friends? Do *I look* for ways to make a positive difference?

Can I see the value of other people's contributions? Do I demean my own role or that of others? Do I look for fault in my team's performance or do I find ways to lift and elevate us to higher ground?

Do I talk about my work with enthusiasm?

Do I often use self-deprecating expressions? "I'm just a…" "My opinion doesn't matter anyway," "Nobody seems to care what I think," "It doesn't even matter if I show up."

How can I elevate my description of what I do in life?

FOCAL POINT
What will I do to promote a sense of higher purpose in my life?

_____
_____
_____
_____
_____
_____
_____
_____
_____
_____

Owners seldom take offense

Seldom take offense/Easily offended

Other people can be offensive, but Owners refuse to take the bait. They refuse to play the part of a wounded Victim; they see that as a big waste of time.

Their dignity stems from their commitment to higher conduct and ideals.

ELEANOR ROOSEVELT

Former First Lady, Eleanor Roosevelt, exemplified the trait of not taking offense. This strong woman continually used her influence to further worthy social causes during the time her husband, Franklin Roosevelt, was President of the United States.

Physically, Eleanor was not an attractive woman and she became the object of many cruel, low-class jokes. Despite the barbs and cruelty she took the high road. Her words have set a tone for many people. She said, "No one can make you feel inferior without your consent."

Victims are easily offended. They're hyper-judgmental. They take offense at the drop of a word or glance. It's almost as though they're looking for slights and disrespect. Because they look for offenses, it doesn't take them long to find them and work themselves into a lather over how thoughtless and evil their perceived offenders are. Consequently, they live in a bitter, unhappy place.

> *"No one can make you feel inferior without your consent."*
>
> *Eleanor Roosevelt*

Owners exhibit greater self-confidence and don't allow errant words to diminish their self-esteem or ability to achieve at high levels. Consider the example of Tiger Woods, one of the most dominant performers in the history of golf.

A while back another professional golfer made a racial slur directed at Tiger Woods. Despite the fact that the other golfer later apologized, Tiger was immediately swarmed by reporters. As the cameras rolled, they launched their questions. "Did you hear what he said about you? What's your response to his comments?" Tiger rose above it all as he stated,

> "At first I was shocked to hear…these unfortunate remarks. His attempt at humor was out of place, and I was disappointed by it. But I've played golf with him, and I know he's a jokester. I have concluded that no personal animosity toward me was intended. I respect him as a golfer, and a person," stated Tiger, "and for the many good things he has done for others throughout his career. I know he feels badly about the remarks. We all make mistakes, and it is time to move on."

Tiger has learned that Owners are not easily offended, and in fact, understand and practice the art of forgiveness, replacing bitterness and self-pity with constructive thought and energy.

PONDER POINTS
Seldom take offense/Easily offended

Do I find myself ruminating on the negative comments others have made about me?

Am I concerned with ideas and goals more than with leadership style and appearance?

Do I constantly worry about what others think and say about me?

Do I expect and look for negative or judgmental comments from others?

How does my choice of thoughts and attitudes amplify or diminish potential offenses in my life?

When was the last time I was offended? Did I respond in a way that prolonged the agony? What would I do differently in a similar situation in the future?

What grudge or bitter feeling am I holding? How is that affecting my perceptions? What can I do to move beyond those feelings?

FOCAL POINT
What will I do to maintain more poise and dignity in my life?

_____
_____
_____
_____
_____
_____
_____
_____
_____
_____

Owners use life

Use life/Used by life

Owners have vision, purposes, plans, and goals.

They sense that they're able to control a good deal of what happens in their life. They use time as the conduit to get where they want to go.

Ask an Owner, "What do you intend to do in the next five years?" The Owner may not have an answer right on the tip of his tongue, but he'll certainly understand the question. He might say something like,

> "Well, I'm not quite sure; I've got lots of options.
> I'm kind of pondering things right now."

Ask a Victim the same question, "How are you going to spend the next five years?" and he'll answer something like this:

> "Well how should I know? It all depends if my wife and children come back."
> "It all depends on whether I get fired or not."

Far from feeling "in charge," Victims feel like life uses them.

Victims see life as a series of attacks and mishaps. Whenever something goes awry, they drag out the word "Life," and berate it. If they get a flat tire on the way to work, they'll revile life, "I was going to be on time. Now this happens. Well, that's life for you." Victims say things like:

> "Never pays to get your hopes up.
> Life will come and kick you right in the teeth, man."

> "Flying high in April, shot down in May."

By repeating such pessimistic language each day, Victims associate life with negativity, sometimes bordering on torture.

Victim-speak contradicts itself. Some Victims will go on and on about how horrible their job is; yet, their worst fear is that they might lose it. If you say to them, "Well, if it's so bad, why don't you just quit?" they'll say, "Because my next job might be even worse!"

Here's a thinking tool that Owners use to stay on the Owner side:

> "How can I use this?"

This question works as a great tool to engage creative thinking, and to take more responsibility. Even amid painful trials you can trigger powerful thoughts by asking yourself, "How can I use this?"

CANDY LIGHTNER

You may not recognize the name Candy Lightner.

Candy's twelve year-old daughter was killed by a drunk driver. As you would expect, she was devastated and she shed many tears. But she also applied a high level of Ownership. She did not live in denial, neither did she vent her rage on the drunk driver. And she didn't become bitter, withdrawn, or sullen. Instead, she asked herself, "How can I use this?"

As she emerged from the grief, she made herself a promise,

> "I refuse to be the second victim of that driver. I am going to do something constructive with this."

Candy Lightner will go to her grave having saved thousands of lives, though she will never know precisely how many. Candy Lightner founded the organization M.A.D.D., Mothers Against Drunk Driving.

Like Candy Lightner, Owners appreciate the value of life—the value of each day. They often reflect on their own talents, abilities and interests, and explore ways to develop them further. They actively seek opportunities in their personal and professional lives to advance a cause, fill a need, or provide a helping hand. Because Owners use life, it becomes a wonderful, fulfilling adventure.

> "Let us resolve to be masters, not the victims, of our history, controlling our own destiny without giving way to blind suspicions and emotions."
>
> *John F. Kennedy*

APPLICATION

Pause for a moment and think about the section you've just read. On the application page (pages 110-111), write down two Victim statements and two Owner statements based on the contrasts just described.

EXAMPLES

Victim Language	Owner Language
Nothing ever goes my way.	How can I make the best of this?
I am so swamped I don't even know where to begin."	I enjoy a good challenge.
My job is leading me nowhere fast.	I've been taking an interesting class on e-commerce and it has already helped me at work.
I am so bored. There's never anything interesting to do.	I just volunteered to help the school with their reading program.
I never have time to do the things I want to do.	I have a lot more energy since I started exercising early every morning.

PONDER POINTS
Use life/Used by life

Do I often feel swamped or overwhelmed?

Do I frequently feel like other people take advantage of me?

Do I have well-defined priorities for myself right now?

Do I take time to plan my days and my months to accomplish what I want to accomplish?

Am I working to achieve meaningful goals in my life?

FOCAL POINT
What is the single most powerful goal that energizes my life right now?

_____
_____
_____
_____
_____
_____
_____
_____
_____
_____

Owners take responsibility

Take responsibility/Shift responsibility

Owners take responsibility—
they look for what to do.

Victims shift responsibility—
they look for what or whom to resent.

Owners are not simply content with getting a job done. They often look for opportunities to go the extra mile in fulfilling assignments. They like to exceed the expectations of others. They appreciate being held accountable for their performance. They solicit feedback and suggestions on how to improve their future performance. They celebrate the success of a job well-done and give credit where credit is due.

When Owners encounter obstacles or setbacks, they learn from the moment and keep looking forward—thinking of their destination, not the predicament. They acknowledge and take responsibility for their mistakes, make course corrections, and press on. They ask themselves useful questions that promote higher creativity in their search for solutions, such as:

"Where do I want to go from here?"
"What needs to be done now?"
"What options do we have?"

By undertaking these kinds of questions, Owners engage their brains in productive pursuits, developing pathways of action. Unfortunately, Victims disable their creative faculties and promote inaction by focusing on their disappointment over the situation. They cling to the vain hope that resenting the circumstances will cause the obstacles to dissolve under the heat of their disdain.

As frustration brews within, Victims fan the flames by justifying why they are not responsible. Thoughts like, "I didn't create this mess, why do I have to fix it?" "It's not my fault that so-and-so didn't see this coming and intercept it," fill their minds. The shifting of responsibility spills over into statements of powerlessness and incapability.

"It's not my job."
"Why does this always happen to me?"
"There's nothing I can do,"

This latter comment is a common deflection and is entirely untrue. *There's always something one can do to help.* Because Owners have learned to assume responsibility for their actions, they do not live with the fear of failure. They are willing to take calculated risks in order to improve their performance. Responsibility and accountability liberate their creativity and fuel their drive. They become solution providers rather than problem finders. And the rewards follow.

PONDER POINTS
Take responsibility/Shift responsibility

When I encounter obstacles and adversity, do I explore options that can produce meaningful resolution or do I look for somebody or something to blame for the problem?

How do I respond to new challenges or assignments? Do I welcome additional responsibility and accountability, or do I try to avoid or shift it?

Do I find more comfort in talking about a problem or in doing something to improve the situation?

When is the last time I volunteered for additional responsibility on a project?

FOCAL POINT
What will I do to assume more responsibility for success and fulfillment in my life?

_____
_____
_____
_____
_____
_____
_____
_____
_____
_____
_____
_____

Owners see themselves as "the programmer"

The programmer/The program

*Owners believe people can change and grow,
and victims tend to doubt it.*

Owners exercise optimism in human possibility and potential, and it makes a huge difference in their lives. Owners believe in continuous self-improvement, take responsibility for it, and look for ways to up-grade their performance.

Fundamentally, Owners see themselves as "the programmer," while Victims see themselves as "the program." Owners pay attention to their self-talk, recognizing that it equates to self-programming.

By contrast, Victims only give lip service to the possibility of real change. They hold that people are who they are, and that everyone needs to accept themselves pretty much as they are. Victims also tend to amplify and overstate their self-descriptions, undermining their own progress by turning an inclination into an identity. Instead of saying, "My game has plateaued at the bogey level," a Victim would say, "I'm a bogey golfer." "I am a bogey golfer" implies that a current stage of progress is a permanently encoded trait that can't be altered or improved.

An Owner would say, "I've decided to work on my people skills. I'm going to get out of my shell and show more concern for other people." A Victim would say, "I'm not a people person. I'm more the reserved type. I'm shy by nature."

> *"If you don't have the power to change yourself, then nothing will change around you."*
>
> — *Anwar al Sadat*

When we think of ourselves as programmers instead of the program, we make a clear separation between the emotion and the self. In a Victim's mind they become entangled and appear to be one and the same. Victims personify with their present patterns of behavior and refer to their moods as though they were their very identity. That is why change seems so difficult and doubtful.

An Owner would say something like, "I'm not in the best of moods right now. I'm feeling frustrated and angry." A Victim would tend to personify, saying, "I am angry" or "I am frustrated."

Personification or identification obscures the simple fact that states of being are a choice, and that we can start them when we want and shut them off when we want.

> *"I was a vegetarian until I started leaning toward the sunlight."*
>
> — *Rita Rudner*

EMOTIONS ARE CREATED

Owners understand that emotions are a creation—a by-product or print-out of the thoughts under their direct control.

Victims think that emotions just happen. They take no responsibility for the birth or death of any mood, implying that emotions depend on outside factors beyond their control. Victims say things like, "I've lost my enthusiasm for the job," suggesting that enthusiasm is an object, like a paper clip, that can be lost or mislaid. Evidently, they expect to be rummaging through a drawer some day and stumble across it again.

> "Well, what do you know? I found my 'enthusiasm for the job.'
> I wondered where I lost it—it must've fallen in here by the stapler."

Another erroneous twist in Victim-thinking implies that emotions have a persona or life of their own. "I've lost my enthusiasm for this job. It went away," insinuating that "enthusiasm," having a brain and a will of its own, thought it over one day, and made the conscious decision to pack up and leave the poor Victim standing there, empty and alone.

Sometimes Victims refer to their moods as though the mood not only had discretionary power to come or go on its own, but that when it arrives, it takes control of the Victim's entire being and behavior.

> "My temper sure gets away from me at times—
> like when I smashed that radio to pieces. That Rush Limbaugh sure
> ticks me off sometimes. Got my temper from my dad, you know.
> All of the men in our family have short fuses—kinda runs in the blood line.
> Yep, sometimes my temper just flares up and gets the best of me."

COMMITMENTS ARE DECISIONS, NOT FEELINGS

Another variation on this theme applies to the all-important subject of commitment. Owners and Victims view commitment very differently.

Owners hold that commitments are a decision—a conscious choice. They can choose to elevate their commitment or withdraw it. Victims view commitment as a feeling—something that comes and goes on its own volition.

> *"I just don't feel as committed to you as I once did. Something's missing. I can't tell you what it is exactly, it's just not there for me any more."*

Victims vacillate. A change of circumstance precipitates a change of commitment. Owners take the opposite approach. They *drive* circumstances and events by the force of their commitments.

Victims give up some of the best things in life because they think "they're too much of a hassle." Their personal relationships waver tenuously on the edge of their feelings instead of the sure footing of their determined efforts. They view love and commitment as though they were as insubstantial and fleeting as stomach gas.

> *"I think I love you. Yes, yes, I definitely feel it.*
> *Oh, wait…wait a second.*
> *No, sorry…it just went away. I guess it's over.*
> *Well, it was nice while it…oh, wait, I think it's coming back!*
> *Yes! Yes, I feel it! I love you after all."*

To Owners, commitments are a matter of integrity, not a matter of whim. We *decide* to be committed to a given person or we choose not to be. We *choose* to commit to the company's goals and initiatives, or we don't. We *make up our mind* to stand for world-class customer service, or to stand for something less. We generate the commitment to "go the extra mile" and astound the customer, or we decide to coast and just "get by."

It's all choice. And, it's all in our power.

APPLICATION

Pause for a moment and think about the section you've just read. On the application page (pages 110-111), write down two Victim statements and two Owner statements based on the contrasts just described.

EXAMPLES

Victim Language	Owner Language
That's just my personality. I've always been this way.	You're right. I see how I can change the way I do that.
That guy drives me crazy!	I've allowed some of his quirks to annoy me. I'm going to focus on some of his positives instead.
I have never been good with math.	I've been working with a tutor who has really helped me understand math.
Hey, I just do what they tell me.	I've been thinking about this, and I have a suggestion.
Well, we tried. It just didn't work out.	We need to get more creative on this one. We're not going to let this setback stop us.
I'm sick and tired.	No, you're just sickening and tiring.

PONDER POINTS
The programmer/The program

In general, am I optimistic or pessimistic about change in myself?

In general, am I optimistic or pessimistic about change in others?

How do I talk about my emotions? Do I personify with the emotion, or do I see the emotion as a choice?

What are my key commitments in life? How do I demonstrate my integrity to my commitments?

Do circumstances drive my commitments, or do my commitments drive my circumstances?

What was my thought-life like today?

FOCAL POINT
What important change do I want to make and how could I measure my progress?

_____
_____
_____
_____
_____
_____
_____

PARTING SHOT

Best-selling author, Steve Chandler—a gifted speaker and trainer—and a strong advocate and practitioner of the Ownership Spirit relates the following personal experience:

> *A while back, my daughter, Stephanie, had gotten to that age where it was cool to be a little bit cynical and negative. Like many teenagers, she'd developed the habit of using one particular victim statement—probably the most popular one among teenagers today. They like this statement because of its "shock value" when used in front of adults. I'm referring to the phrase, "Life sucks."*
>
> *When things didn't go Stephanie's way, I'd hear her mutter that phrase, and I'd tried several different approaches in an effort to get her to stop saying it, to no avail.*
>
> *One day, after a particularly trying day, I suppose, Stephanie came home from school, slammed her books on the table and said, "It's just like I said, Dad, life sucks!" I calmly disagreed, and responded,*
>
> *"No, Stephanie, life doesn't suck. YOUR life sucks."*

Indeed, in life there are Owners and there are Victims. Moment by moment, we stand at mental crossroads choosing one or the other. Our life's creation will be the result of the conscious decisions we make at those crossroads. As the great philosopher Johann Wolfgang von Goethe said, *"Each has his own happiness in his hands, as the artist handles the rude clay he seeks to reshape it into a figure; yet it is the same with this art as with all others: only the capacity for it is innate; the art itself must be learned and painstakingly practiced."*

We invite you to pay the price and enjoy the journey of transforming Victim-thinking into Owner-thinking and reap the benefits of The Ownership Spirit.

TRANSFORMING VICTIM HABITS

As you've studied the contrasts in Owner/Victim thinking, hopefully you have detected some Victim habits or tendencies. If so, you're ready to employ a simple three-step method for transforming those unproductive phrases into productive ones.

First: Identify Victim Statement

When you notice a Victim statement in your thinking or speech, write it down. This helps in two ways. First, the emphasis sharpens your awareness, making it easier to "catch" the thought in the future. Second, you can rescript the thought and "program" a better alternative.

Second: Determine an Owner Alternative

Once you've identified a Victim thought, think of a few productive substitutes or alternatives. Write these down as well. Then select the best one.

Third: Look for Opportunities to Redirect Thinking

Stay alert. When you catch yourself thinking the Victim thought, redirect your thinking to the more constructive Owner thought. With a little repetition, you'll soon notice that the Owner thought will replace the weaker one almost automatically.

EXERCISE

Refer back to the Victim part of the Self Recognition Exercise on page 57 of this book. Write down the Victim statements that are checked "Often" on the form to the right on the Victim side of the ledger. Select an Owner statement as a substitute for each one. Review the list from time to time. Rehearse replacing the Victim statement with the Owner statement that you have chosen. It won't take long for the Owner thoughts to become habit.

TRANSFORMATION TOOL

Victim	Owner

Example:

Victim Statement
If only I hadn't…

Owner Statement
Where do I want to go from here?

RECOMMENDATIONS FOR INCREASED OWNERSHIP

First: Carry a Reminder.

Create a tangible, visible "Owner/Victim Reminder" to serve as a means of re-triggering awareness.

Quma Learning has minted a Owner/Victim medallion that can be carried in a pocket, purse, or planner. About the size and weight of a traditional U.S. silver dollar, this tangible icon has a large "O" on one side and a "V" on the other — the Owner side smooth and the Victim side rough. People carry the medallion as means of maintaining awareness, reminding them to choose better thought patterns.

Second: Hold a daily journaling session.

If you haven't done so already, establish a daily journaling habit. Journaling is the semi-formal procedure of recording events, insights, and "lessons learned" on a daily basis. The benefits of this habit are myriad. When we pause to think, assess, and evaluate, we draw more value from each day's experience, making personal discoveries and capturing insights that would have otherwise slipped away.

Among other benefits, journaling affords a golden opportunity to keep the Ownership Spirit thriving. As you pause to replay the events of your day, think about the Owner/Victim equation and ask yourself,

> "In what moments did I act like an Owner?
> In what moments did I act like a Victim?"

This self-assessment session ensures continual growth and awareness.

Third: Enroll coaches

Even Tiger Woods has a coach. As proficient as he is—unquestionably one of the best in his profession—Tiger knows that a supportive pair of external eyes can see things that he can't. Enroll your spouse, roommate, or significant other as a coach to help you recognize moments when you're applying Owner traits and when you aren't.

At work, many work teams have created a mutual-coaching environment. Members of the team agree to coach one another in applying the principles and methods outlined in the handbook.

Quma's website, www.quma.net, also offers tips and tools to use in applying the Ownership Spirit.

> "We are what we repeatedly do.
> Excellence, then, is not an act, but a habit."
>
> *Aristotle*

OWNER STATEMENTS

Independent
_____
_____
_____

By Choice
_____
_____
_____

Get From
_____
_____
_____

Higher Purpose
_____
_____
_____

Seldom Take Offense
_____
_____
_____

Use Life
_____
_____
_____

Takes Responsibility
_____
_____
_____

The Programmer
_____
_____
_____

VICTIM STATEMENTS

Dependent

Against Will

Get Through

Lower Purpose

Easily Offended

Used by Life

Shifts Responsibility

The Program

> "The other day I got out my can-opener and was opening a can of worms when I thought 'What am I doing?'!"
>
> *Jack Handy*
> Deep thoughts from "Saturday Night Live"

Tough-Minded Ownership

Writing the Software of Tough-Minded Thinking

Tough-Minded Ownership Objectives

Acquire the superior rewards that stem from up-grading mental software and operating systems

Apply insights from the most reputable research on the thought processes of highly productive people

Understand the leading factors that determine resilience and persistence, and why some people quit and others don't

Identify one's personal explanatory style (through a self-assessment test)

Study the traits and develop habits of Tough-Minded Ownership

Tough-Minded Ownership
Writing the Software of Tough-Minded Thinking

Table of Contents

114	Tough-Minded Ownership Objectives
117	The Incomparable Human Biocomputer
120	Mental Viruses
123	Re-Writing the "Because…therefore" Virus
127	The "I am my personality" Virus
133	The Seligman Research: Learned Optimism
139	Developing Tough-Minded Ownership
145	Traits of Tough-Minded Owners
150	About Quma Learning

The
Incomparable Human Biocomputer

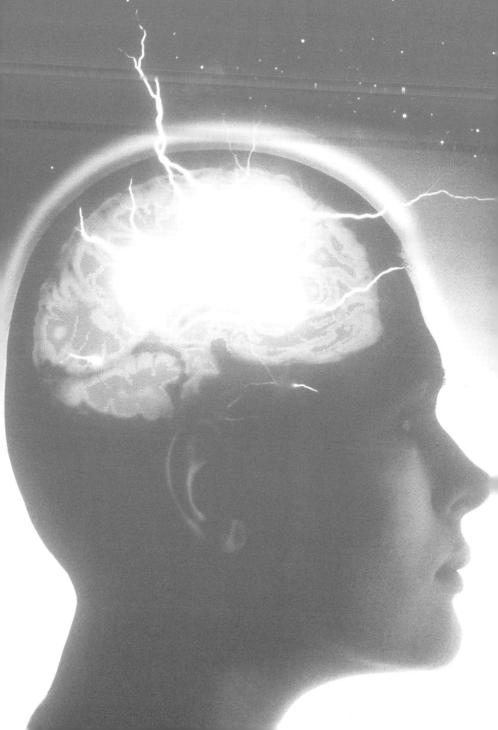

THE COMPUTER THAT EXCELS ALL COMPUTERS

Throughout this trilogy of Ownership Spirit handbooks, we have invited you to engage in the most rigorous, challenging, and exciting course work any human being can engage in. The demands of this undertaking exceed any technical or so-called "hard skills" training on the planet. The challenge: successfully programming and operating the incomparable Human Biocomputer—our own brains. Consider for a moment some of this computer's astounding features and capabilities:

The human biocomputer is the only computer that can spontaneously repair its own circuits. Of course, the brain can be injured beyond the point of recovery, yet within reasonably broad margins, the brain has an impressive ability to heal itself and reroute damaged circuits, as in the case of a stroke. No other computer possesses such self-healing capability.

Second, it's the only computer that writes its own software. Each person wields sovereign control over his or her own mental keyboard—no one else has access to it. In the exclusive inner zone of our thought processes, we alone make the keystrokes that determine who we are and what we do, making the choices that decide everything from our attitudes to our actions. No outside force or entity can assume, usurp, or exercise this prerogative. Thinking is a completely individual process—you write your software, and I write mine.

WE SET OUR OWN THERMOSTATS

Although we live in a generation when many people flatly refuse to accept responsibility for their character or characteristics, careful analysis and reason give us no place to hide. When all is said and done, the source of our shortcomings resides in the software we've designed and forged into habits.

We are even responsible for the duration and intensity of our own temptations. Some people balk at that idea and say, "It's not my fault if the media keeps throwing all these alluring temptations at me." True, we may not be able to control the *presentation* of enticing images to our minds, but we do control *how long they linger*. When a dessert commercial invites me to break my commitment to cut back on sweets, I'm still in the driver's seat. The temptation lasts only as long as I allow my mind to dwell on that particular image. If I choose to focus on the dessert and imagine its tastes and textures beguiling my palate, the intensity of the temptation grows. On the other hand, if I reject the invitation and put my mind on something else, the temptation is essentially ended the moment I take control and direct my thoughts to another subject. As the country sage observed, "You can't keep a bird from landing on your head, but you don't have to let it build a nest there."

Temptations often stem from images presented from the outside, but we, and we alone, determine what we'll do with them.

Ideas and impulses are continually presented to our minds, but we decide whether we'll embrace or reject them. We alone decide the subject and tone of our thoughts. Thus, moment by moment, we're running our life on the software program that we ourselves have written.

Here's another amazing property: As the biocomputer writes its software, it can expand its own hardware. When we acquire new information, a new circuit forms in the cortex of our brain, literally and physically. If we repeat the idea with some regularity, more cells join the circuit, making it more prominent and usable. Each new circuit has the capacity to form new connections with tens of thousands of other circuits, thus increasing our brain power and mental capability. The more we learn and the harder we work our brains, the more creative and capable we become. Think of the possibilities that property affords us.

Additionally, the human biocomputer is the only computer that can alter the course of events by its own volition. It can willfully, intentionally impact the outside world, determining outcomes and instigating changes by simply deciding to do so.

Self-Healing

Writes Its Own Software

Expands Its Own Hardware (Circuits)

Alters Outcomes & Events

The brain works a lot like a muscle—the harder you use it, the more it grows…The brain has a remarkable capacity to change and grow, even in old age, and individuals have some control over how healthy and alert their brains remain as years go by.

Daniel Golden
Science Editor, Newsweek Magazine

Now we come to a provocative question:

Can the human biocomputer be afflicted with viruses?

The answer "yes" is correct on two levels. First, on a purely physical level, biological viruses can multiply and cause damage to brain tissue, as in the case of meningitis or encephalitis. Second, on the mental level, we can be impaired by the presence of detrimental "code" in our thought processes.

Mental viruses often prove to be more harmful than physical ones, and far more difficult to diagnose and treat. Troubleshooting mental viruses presents a formidable challenge because, although it's entirely unintentional, we have all authored sections of code that don't serve us well and impede our progress. In fact, the biggest challenge in operating the human biocomputer comes down to this very issue—the elimination of viruses—because only one entity on earth can troubleshoot and execute a mental virus. That entity is the selfsame computer that wrote the virus in the first place.

Only we can troubleshoot our own self-written viruses. The computer that wrote the virus has to elevate its awareness to the point that it can recognize that the code which it has written is defective or detrimental and then re-write new code to improve and replace it. Then, it has to maintain awareness long enough to repeat the new code with sufficient frequency that it will be accepted as the preferred circuit and become the new default!

When it comes to mental viruses, only the computer that wrote the virus can troubleshoot it.

*Thought is the real causative force in life,
and there is no other. You cannot have one kind
of mind and another kind of environment.
If you change your mind, your conditions must
change too—your body must change, your activities
must change, your home must change, the color-tone
of your whole life must change.*

*This may be called the Great Cosmic Law.
The practical difficulty in applying it arises from the
fact that our thoughts are so close to us that it is difficult,
without a little practice, to stand back and look at them
objectively. Yet that is just what you must do. You must
train yourself to choose the subject of your thinking at
any given time, and also to choose the emotional tone.*

Emmet Fox
Alter Your Life

Re-Writing the "Because...therefore" Virus

When distortions and exaggerations become automatic and habitual, they amount to viruses in our system

RE-WRITING EXERCISE

As both an illustration of the foregoing points and a skill-building exercise, consider the following:

The "Because…therefore" Virus

Living in an imperfect world, we can't go through a day without experiencing some potentially upsetting events. Although we are capable of thinking reasonably about them, we sometimes select unreasonable distortions and make unfavorable exaggerations. When those distortions and exaggerations become automatic and habitual, they amount to viruses in our system.

A common example of such distortions is the "Because…therefore" line of thinking in which the thinker leaps to unwarranted negative judgments about himself. A statement that follows this pattern is, "My daughter won't keep her room clean. What kind of a parent am I?"

Because: *My daughter doesn't keep her room tidy*
Therefore: *I'm a horrible parent.*

Do you see the glaring incongruence in this logic? To an impartial jury, an unmade bed with some magazines, socks, and sneakers lying around wouldn't amount to irrefutable evidence that you belong in the Parenting Hall of Shame, but that's essentially the only "logical" conclusion this thinker's been able to reach.

Here's another one:

Because: *Business is down for the second quarter in a row.*
Therefore: *I'm just not a good manager.*

Again, the conclusion doesn't fit the "evidence". The trouble with this thinking is that it delays action on the real issue. Sales are more likely to improve when the manager, instead of spending time on self-defamation, ponders the question, "What can we do to boost sales?"

RE-WRITING EXERCISE

We can overcome the "Because...therefore" virus by replacing it with better code—thoughts that can help us acknowledge imperfect results without condemning our value or diminishing our self-worth. "Even though...nevertheless" thinking provides a more realistic and useful train of thought and a good functional remedy for the virus.

Even though: *Our sales are down,*
  Nevertheless: *I'm going to help the team stay focused, creative, and committed to finding new ways of reaching our goals.*

Even though: *Things aren't perfect at home and Suzy could keep her room a lot cleaner,*
  Nevertheless: *I'm going to keep things in perspective and show Suzy more appreciation for the things she does do around the house.*

APPLICATION:

For the next few days, take special note of events that have the potential for ruffling your feathers. For each event, create a specific "Even though...nevertheless" response and note the impact it has on your energy and results. We recommend you follow the format suggested in the form below to reinforce the learning.

Re-Writing the "Because...therefore" Virus

The Event – *Even though:* _____
_____
_____

My Response – *Nevertheless:* _____
_____
_____

The Impact or Result _____
_____
_____

RE-WRITING THE "BECAUSE...THEREFORE" VIRUS

The Event – *Even though:*
_____
_____
_____

My Response – *Nevertheless:*
_____
_____
_____

The Impact or Result
_____
_____
_____
_____

The Event – *Even though:*
_____
_____
_____

My Response – *Nevertheless:*
_____
_____
_____

The Impact or Result
_____
_____
_____

The "I am my personality" Virus

What if we didn't have a personality?

What if we didn't have a personality?

When we delve into the subject of eliminating mental viruses, almost immediately we come to realize that we can be dealing with compound viruses. Some viruses mask and protect other viruses, inhibiting removal by overlying and preventing access to the other ones. For example, we frequently hear phrases such as "I am who I am, and that's all there is to it," "I've got to be me, and I can't be a phony," and "You can't teach an old dog new tricks." With our elevated awareness of mind management principles, we can see that such patterns are not only viruses in and of themselves, but they keep people from taking aim on a host of other self-limiting patterns of thought.

If, for instance, we continually tell ourselves that "Old habits are hard to break," according to The Othello Principle, what will we "look for" and what will we "see?" Habits will become hard to break—harder than they need to be.

Granted, there are no quick fixes. Most of us don't change long-standing habits in the blink of an eye, but neither are we permanently locked into one set pattern of behavior. Habits are only habits. They are acquired behavior, and virtually any acquired behavior can be altered, improved or replaced. But, for many, the principal obstacle to continuous growth and improvement is the erroneous notion that "It's just my personality, and I can't do anything about it."

> *"There are no optimistic or pessimistic personalities; there are only single, individual choices of optimistic or pessimistic thoughts."*
>
> *Steve Chandler*
> *100 Ways to Motivate Yourself*

TARI'S STORY

A fun, outgoing woman by the name of Tari shared part of her life story in one of our seminars. As she told of her school days, she said:

> *"For many years I was the classic 'wall-flower.' I was absolutely petrified of people and I actually tried to avoid them."*

As you can imagine, she didn't have too many friends and she wasn't very happy.

> *"I was miserable," she said,*
> *"but I just didn't know what to do about it."*

Part way through her junior year, Tari's father came home from work with what he thought would be bad news. "I've been transferred," he explained. "We're moving out of state." To Tari, this actually came as good news. She said, "Contrary to the old adage, 'You never get a second chance to make a first impression,' I felt that I did. I was going to a new school. Nobody knew me. I had no reputation to live up to or, in my case, live down to. I felt like I could turn over a new leaf and be someone different than I'd been.

> *"When I entered my new school, I made myself climb*
> *out of my shell. I made myself greet and talk to people.*
> *At first I felt awkward, but gradually I became more confident.*
> *In my final year of school, I actually worked up the courage to*
> *run for a class office, and to my amazement, I won!"*

THE DETERMINANT

What was the fundamental determinant that "produced" Tari, the shy, awkward introvert and Tari, the gregarious, outgoing extrovert? Choice! Innately, she's neither of those personalities—neither an introvert or an extrovert. In essence, she is free to invent whatever version of introversion or extroversion software she chooses. She can be either one or neither one.

No one has a fixed, unchangeable personality! We write and re-rewrite our personal behavioral software anytime we really want to. The notion that we're born with a certain, unchangeable set of codes and are thereby fated to remain forever locked into a given disposition or personality is a self-limiting myth. Character can be developed. Skills can be learned. Traits can be altered. We can change and improve, and we do change and improve, any time we set our mind to it.

When we make the decision, we can shift our mood or disposition within seconds, and we can maintain that posture for as long as we want.

Use your imagination with these next two examples:

Example One

The door bell rings and a ten-year old son answers the door. In a moment he walks back into the room and says to his father, "There's someone at the door who wants to see you. I think he said his name was IRS"

Instantly, a transformation occurs—one that affects the father's mood, demeanor, and physical posture. Shifting from a relaxed, amiable newspaper-reader, he strides to the door exhibiting a certain formal, rather stiff-spined "personality," and in his most business-like manner, he says, "Yes sir, may I help you."

Example Two

A few minutes later, the door bell rings again, and the same son answers the door. In a moment he walks back into the room and says to his father, "There's someone at the door who wants to see you. She says she thinks you're awesome and really wants to meet you. I think she said her name was Cindy Crawford."

In milliseconds another notable transformation occurs, and the "personality" that goes to the door is gracious, warm, and charming, nothing at all like the person who just spoke with the tax collector.

We reinvent ourselves—change our personalities—at will, on the spot, and we do it all the time. If we do it in simple, transient moments, we can do it on a broader scale as well.

For many, the principal obstacle to continuous growth and improvement is the erroneous notion that "I am who I am. It's just my personality, and I can't do anything about it."

The Seligman Research

Learned Optimism

*Why should we bother to learn
to think optimistically?*

We've all established patterns of thought and behavior that have become part of our way of living life. Initially, they weren't automatic patterns, they were just single choices—something we tried out among an array of possible alternatives. By repetition, we've grown comfortable with these choices and we've stayed with them. Now they're habits. Sometimes we become so attached to our habits that we completely identify with them, losing sight of the separation between who we are and what habits we've formed.

Notice the language of identification or personification in phrases like, "I'm a procrastinator," "He's shy," "She's picky," and "I'm a worry-wart." To the biocomputer that kind of language implies permanence. Habits can be changed, but if we think *we are the habit*, we freeze our progress.

Opinions about the degree and magnitude of real change vary widely. Some people doubt that humans can really alter their ways. Obviously, the first step on the road to improvement is to believe that improvement is possible.

In answer to the question, "Can a leopard change its spots?" we turn to the work of Martin E. P. Seligman. Dr. Seligman's investigations comprise some of the most extensive studies ever done on human behavior, involving over twenty years and one thousand studies. The following statement, taken from his book, *The Optimistic Child*, summarizes his work:

> Why should we bother to learn to think optimistically? Isn't pessimism just a posture with no real effects? Unfortunately not. I have studied pessimism for the last twenty years and in more than one thousand studies, involving more than half a million children and adults, pessimistic people do worse than optimistic people in three ways: First, they get depressed much more often. Second, they achieve less at school, on the job, and on the playing field—much less than their talents would suggest. Third, their physical health is worse than that of optimists. So holding a pessimistic theory of the world may be the mark of sophistication, but it is a costly one.

Notice the first sentence. It doesn't say, "Why is it important to be born optimistic?" Though people may be born with a certain traits and tendencies, their deficiencies and propensities are not permanently embedded.

Quite the opposite.

Dr. Seligman and his team reached two main conclusions: First, optimism makes people more effective than pessimism. Optimists achieve and accomplish more. They get more mileage out of every capability, talent, and resource than people whose thoughts are less constructive. That's the point! None of this is about fuzzy, feel-good fluff; it's about elevating performance and getting better results.

The second conclusion is equally powerful: Optimism can be learned. It's not about whether we're born one way or another; it comes down to applied intelligence!

Parents can only give good advice or put [children] on the right paths, but the final forming of a person's character lies in their own hands.

Anne Frank,
Anne Frank: The Diary of a Young Girl, July 15, 1944.

WE ARE NOT OUR HABITS

No one is a born optimist or a born pessimist. No one—by nature, or by genetic code, or by up-bringing and environment—is hopelessly engraved with any given pattern of behavior. Our character and our traits are print-outs of our self-selected and most often repeated thought habits. And, that's all they are. Again, they're just habits.

Reinforced by nothing more than repetition, our habits dictate what seems natural and normal, and differentiates what seems unnatural and abnormal. For example, to a man who has grown up in the United States, driving on the right side of the street seems normal and natural. If he were transferred to London or Singapore, he'd find that all of that could shift in a matter of a few weeks. The first time he drove around London, he'd have to be extremely alert and attentive. Everything about driving would seem strange and awkward. With persistence, however, things would change. If he drove on the left every day for an hour or two, within a week his comfort level would improve. After a couple of months, he'd have the new system mastered and would be quite as comfortable and capable under the new set of rules as with the original.

*That which we persist in doing becomes easier,
not that the nature of the thing has changed,
but our ability to do it has increased.*

Ralph Waldo Emerson

Sow a thought, and you reap an act;
Sow an act, and you reap a habit;
Sow a habit, and you reap a character;
Sow a character, and you reap a destiny.

Samuel Smiles
1812-1904, Life and Labor

Developing Tough-Minded Ownership

*The kind of critical thinking that adds value
draws amperage from the turbine of ownership, not cynicism*

A STEREOTYPE THAT DOESN'T SERVE US

We now focus on the development of Tough-Minded Ownership. A bit of definition work is in order.

Unfortunately, in our society, the title "tough-minded" has been claimed by some people who don't deserve it. According to the popular, but erroneous, stereotype, if you can cut people to ribbons with a few snide swipes of your verbal sword, or dump doubt on plans and proposals with a tone of clever ridicule, then you're intellectually superior, cool, and sophisticated.

Entwined in this stereotype is the notion that if you're positive or optimistic you're an airhead—a mental canary, unsophisticated, and naïve. Truly tough-minded people, you see, are the opposite of giddy cheerleaders; they're gritty, no-nonsense "realists." This type of a "realism" would never be "duped by the cotton candy" some people (who they disdain) build their lives on. In their book, if you're really in touch with reality, you can't help but see that the world is a cold, cruel, disappointing place:

> "It's a dog-eat-dog world out there, Virginia, and you'd better get used to it. There's no such thing as a happy endings. That's just Hollywood malarkey, brewed up to bilk the sappy masses."

If you can cut people to ribbons with a few snide swipes of your verbal sword, you are considered cool and sophisticated.

CRITICAL VS. HYPERCRITICAL

Nobody's advocating shallow thinking or naïveté here, but those who dismiss ownership and optimism as mindlessness are throwing the baby out with the bath water.

Moreover, unchecked cynicism requires no exceptional skill or brain power or toughness. More intellectual and creative effort are required to design and build a skyscraper than tear one down. Too often those who pride themselves on being independent critical thinkers fail to notice that they're not actually thinking, they're just being critical.

The kind of critical thinking that adds value draws amperage from the turbine of ownership, not cynicism. It's willing to undertake probing analysis and energetic thinking precisely because it believes that solutions to daunting challenges can be found.

Cynicism isn't critical thinking, it's *hypercritical* thinking, and it undermines itself. It quickly runs out of energy and gives up without even trying, because it attempts to draw power from inherently weak sources—doubt and pessimism.

*Too often those who pride themselves
on being independent critical thinkers fail
to notice that they're not actually thinking,
they're just being critical.*

UNMASKING CYNICISM

Although cynics, doubters, and pessimists like to pawn themselves off as tough-minded, they have no legitimate claim to the title. They aren't tough at all; they're just lazy. When you get right down to it, they're also quitters. They're the first ones to give up on a problem—the first ones to quit on their thinking—the first ones to withdraw from the fray and bail-out in a tough situation. They say stuff like, "Give it up, man, you'll never budge that. This organization will never change. You're delusional. Pull your head out of the clouds and get real." That kind of an approach requires no effort, no commitment, and no tenacity. Where's the toughness?

In actuality, it takes more tough-mindedness to be an owner than a critic. By far. Owners are the ones who stay focused on a problem and keep their thinking going until they find or invent a solution. Owners are the ones who persist and toil against formidable opposition until they overcome. Owners are the ones who keep racking their brains, applying their minds to make things better, even in the midst of callous adversity. Owners are the ones who set and pursue daunting goals and keep striving until they make headway and prevail.

The people who've made real differences throughout the annals of human history have not been naïve and neither have they been hard-core, doubt-laden "realists." They've been people who've believed in possibility, owned an indomitable spirit, and expended impressive amounts of energy derived from the incomparable mindset of Tough-Minded Ownership!

WHO QUITS AND WHO PERSISTS?

The good news is that there's lots of good news (for all of us). Cynics can change, and everyone of us can move up the scale from where we are to something even better.

Believe it or not, a person's ability to face adversity and triumph over setbacks can be predicted, and weakness in that area can be turned into strength. The faulty code that comprises the "I give up. Why try?" Virus can be rewritten.

ATTRIBUTION THEORY

Misfortune and setbacks happen to everyone. Some people rebound quickly, others don't. Dr. Bernard Weiner of UCLA studied why some people bounce back while others bog down or break down. Originally called "Attribution Theory," these insights are now referred to as "Explanatory Style."

The value in studying explanatory styles rests on one sound premise: In order to make sense of the various events that happen in life, people develop habits of determining cause or affixing meaning to those events. When something happens, good or bad, we explain it to ourselves—reconciling the effects by attributing them to some cause. When those explanations are strong and constructive, adverse circumstances appear less daunting and difficult. Conversely, when explanations are distorted and weak, problems seem to be more perplexing and irresolvable.

A person's ability to face adversity and triumph over setbacks can be predicted, and weakness in that area can be turned into strength.

EXPLANATORY STYLES ARE NOT CREATED EQUAL

The scientists who have delved into this subject have concluded that explanatory style constitutes a key indicator of a person's ability to deal with adversity. Simply put, resilient, persistent people have developed strong explanatory styles, and people who struggle with setbacks have unknowingly formed weak ones.

The second thing authorities in this area have concluded is that no one's explanatory pattern is irrevocably embedded. People can strengthen and improve thier style. All it takes is a bit of awareness and practice.

*The only habits we cannot change
are the habits we do not see.*

*Your habitual way of explaining bad events,
your explanatory style, is more than just the words
you mouth when you fail. It is a habit of thought, learned
in childhood and adolescence…It is the hallmark of whether
you are an optimist or pessimist.*

Martin E. P. Seligman, PhD.

Traits of Tough-Minded Owners

Even when they encounter bone-jolting adversity, owners stay committed to their commitments.

To accelerate our acquisition of the rewards and benefits enjoyed by tough-minded owners, it pays to study their qualities and emulate them. Among their traits, five significant mindsets stand out.

1. Tough-Minded Owners Are Undaunted by Difficulty

Nobody is exempt. We all experience trials and adversity. Tough-minded people accept that fact. Consequently, they're not surprised, shocked, or dismayed when things don't go their way and they encounter difficulty. It's not that they go *looking for* it. They just know that adversity is part of the territory, and everyone has their share.

Hard-boiled pessimists, on the other hand, go to one of two extremes. They either claim clairvoyant omniscience by saying, "I knew it wouldn't work," or they seem to be absolutely stunned and amazed when things go wrong. "I can't believe that happened," they say, as though some unwritten law in the universe states that life's supposed to conform to their wishes. "It says right here in Section 17, paragraph 4: 'I'm supposed to be coddled and spoon fed.' So why's all this stuff happening to me?"

Tough-minded owners understand that life is about growth, and that a lot of that growth comes from handling problems and overcoming adversity. They accept one of the great laws of nature: All living things follow the pattern of the butterfly emerging from the cocoon—they're *strengthened by struggle*.

Living things are strengthened by struggle.

2. Tough-Minded Owners Are Willing to Divide in Order to Conquer

Frequently, pessimists get trapped in an "all-or-nothing" mindset. If they can't snap their fingers and dismiss a problem in one brief instant, they throw up their hands and quit. "Ah, stop kidding yourself. You'll never change that; you're not being realistic."

A stronger mindset builds on the idea that sometimes a war has to be won one battle at a time. Gene Krantz, former head of mission control at NASA, exemplified this trait during the ill-fated Apollo 13 mission, when things went dramatically wrong. In a literal case of life-or-death, mission control faced a truly daunting list of dilemmas which, when viewed in aggregate, seemed impossible to solve. For Krantz's team, Gene's stirring words, "Failure is not an option!" became the rallying cry that kept their minds focused on breaking the situation down, attacking one issue at a time. Working under tremendous time pressure, they solved each problem, one by one, resulting in the safe return of three very grateful astronauts, Lovell, Haise, and Swigert, back to earth.

3. Tough Minded Owners Heighten Their Creative Energy

Some people think creativity is binary, "you either have it or you don't." Tough-minded owners understand that not only can creativity be developed, it can be elevated by intention. One simple and powerful technique for heightening creative energy is to dream big! When we commit to something lofty or extraordinary it turns on the juices and our minds become more alert, active, and inventive.

Pessimistic thinking stifles energy and creativity. Literally. It's no more complicated than that. If you want to put some zest into your life, raise the bar of your expectations, fully commit to making something outrageous happen, and watch what it does to your energy and your creativity.

*When it comes to controlling our minds,
attempting to repress a thought—trying not to think it—
backfires every time. It simply does not work.
The key is to shift subject matter.
Focus on a more constructive topic.
You don't overcome thoughts, you replace them.*

4. Tough Minded Owners Redirect Their Negative Thoughts

The stereotypical assumption is that some people just naturally think positively and others negatively, when in fact a lot of tough-minded owners have about as many negative impulses occur to their minds as hard-core pessimists. No one has any inborn "mental immunity." The actual difference is that owners refuse to dwell at great lengths on the negative side of the equation. They learn to flip the coin over and engage their thinking on possibilities rather than restrictions. And, here's how they do it: they redirect instead of repress.

The conscious mind has a unique characteristic that scientists call "lateral or peripheral inhibition," which means that we're designed to have a "one track mind." Although we are aware of a lot of things on the periphery, we can only focus on one thing at a time. So, trying not to think a certain thought is the surest way to rivet your attention on it. That approach simply does not work. What does work is to give your mind an alternative—some other place to go.

To get rid of a negative thought, you supplant or replace it with something more constructive and useful. *Redirect, don't repress.*

5. Tough Minded Owners Alter Circumstances by Their Commitments

Mastering this mindset signifies attainment of the graduate level of tough-minded ownership. This is the apex, and no one attains it in a moment, but the rewards and pay-offs are enormous. People possessing this state of mind make things happen that otherwise would not have happened, being a cause rather than an effect.

Lesser mindsets tend to give in to circumstance more easily, sometimes almost readily. In the face of resistance, instead of maintaining steadfast commitment, they turn to explanations. For some people it's an immediate, almost reflexive, response. They set a goal and begin to move forward. Then, the moment something unfavorable occurs and they encounter a setback, they relinquish their grip on their goal and seek to justify their lack of attainment by reporting on as many mitigating circumstances as possible. In essence, circumstances become the cause and their results become the effects.

Truly tough-minded owners are not willing to settle and they re-double their efforts. As they do so, it's not unusual for them to discover sources of strength that they didn't know they had—sources that those who throw in the towel quickly never find.

Nobody is saying that owners never fail. They do. Regularly. Sometimes circumstances and events defeat them (temporarily). But they never go down without ferocious effort. Tough-minded optimists are battlers and they're tenacious. They keep striving and thinking creatively, even when the outlook dims and things grow bleak. They'll say, "Well, we didn't expect that to happen, but it's still not too late. What do we have to do now to still make this work?"

Tough-minded owners stick to their commitments, even when it's inconvenient or downright painful. They forge ahead, knowing that many times amazing things happen at the eleventh hour and the fifty-ninth minute.

EXCEPTIONAL EFFORT NEVER GOES UNREWARDED

On some occasions, even after working to the eleventh hour, the fifty-ninth minute and the fifty-ninth second, tough-minded owners still fall short. On this day, they were not able to make it happen. Nevertheless, because they have worked and battled without giving up—right up to the last moment—they have gained something that can't be obtained any other way. They will have developed mental, moral, spiritual, creative, and experiential muscle that will give them greater power over circumstance and events in the coming days. Eventually they become so powerful that their states of mind have such authority that circumstances conform to their will with little or no variance. Nothing can stop them.

QUMA LEARNING SYSTEMS, INC.

For two decades, Quma Learning has maintained a steadfast commitment to human development. Our principle-based teachings, coupled with a wide variety of practical, application-enhancing tools, give people the resources they need to achieve more in their lives by improving their thinking processes.

Quma Learning provides instructor-led and computer-based training, along with customized learning tools, to hundreds of thousands of people in over eight languages throughout the world. We work with businesses and corporations, large and small, including many of the Fortune 500, as well as individuals, governmental organizations, educational institutions and charitable foundations, assisting people to stretch their capabilities, accelerate their performance, and reach their visions, goals and objectives.

We invite you to visit our web site at **www.quma.net**, or to call **1-800-622-6463**.